Richard Luck

The Pocket Essential

SAM PECKINPAH

www.pocketessentials.com

First published in Great Britain 2000 by Pocket Essentials, 18 Coleswood Road, Harpenden, Herts, AL5 1EQ

Distributed in the USA by Trafalgar Square Publishing, P.O. Box 257, Howe Hill Road, North Pomfret, Vermont 05053

A CIP catalogue record for this book is available from the British Library.

ISBN 1-903047-20-X

9 8 7 6 5 4 3 2 1

Book typeset by Lies
Printed and bound by Cox & Wyman

for Mum and Dad
and Jim and Emma
and Andy and Dan
and Brett and Brad

Acknowledgements

The interviews in this book were conducted at the University of California, San Diego (1993/4) and The National Film Theatre, London (1995). Many thanks to everyone who participated. Thanks also to John Ashbrook for his generosity and friendship, and to Paul Duncan for making sure that this old hack will ride off into the sunset happy.

Contents

Sam Peckinpah: The Last Outlaw

Film critics can be quite lazy people. I know this for a fact since I spent most of 1996 eating cold Pop Tarts and watching John Landis movies. Eating lukewarm snack foods while watching ho-hum comedies is one of the more palatable forms of film writer's sloth, however. For truly unattractive forms of laziness, you need look no further than the tendency of critics to describe directors using a single word. You know the score: Stanley Kubrick is 'meticulous,' Terry Gilliam is 'quirky,' Paul Schrader is 'Bressonian' and Robert Bresson is 'austere.' Of course, one word is all you need to describe the work of some film-makers (Stanley Kramer: 'worthy,' Joel Schumacher: 'shite'). But Kubrick, Gilliam and Co. don't suit simplification at all well. Nor does Sam Peckinpah, a man whom idle hacks have made synonymous with the word 'bloody.' Of course, there's no disguising the fact that Peckinpah's pictures are packed with corpuscles. Blimey, some are completely swimming in red stuff. But Sam's films are drenched with other things, too. They're packed with contradiction and certainty, camaraderie and betrayal, redemption and revenge, melancholy and joy, shrieking violence and merciful tenderness.

They're steeped in sincerity, too. You see, Sam's films weren't about the way he thought life should be; they were about the way he lived his life. By the same turn, he wasn't just someone who made films about bandits, he really was a bandit. He even said as much: "The outlaws of the old West have always fascinated me. I suppose I'm a bit of an outlaw myself."

Sam's gunslinging lifestyle consisted of equal parts brawling and boozing. He snorted his way through a blizzard of cocaine and bedded prostitutes in vast numbers. He wore symbols of machismo like the bandanna and the mirror shades as if they were medals of honour. Yep, Sam had the lasciviousness, psychosis and swagger of the men he made movies about, but he also had their keen work ethic, their high regard for loyalty and their appreciation of the positive affects of male camaraderie. Oh yes, *and* he was one of the greatest artists of the 20th century. Indeed, I would bet my mortal soul that in a hundred years people will be talking about Sam Peckinpah the way we now talk about great American authors like Ernest Hemingway and Herman Melville.

David Samuel Peckinpah was born on February 21 1925 in Fresno, the cherry-picking capital of California. It's hard to reconcile the young Sam with the hard-drinking whore fucker of his later years. Shy and gawky, Peckinpah wasn't at all suited to life in the America wilds. His self-consciousness must have been made all the more painful by the presence of rugged outdoors men like his lawyer father David Snr. Although he preferred haiku to hunting, the adolescent Sam pursued the same hobbies, if not the same profession, as his dad. He so embraced the mountain man lifestyle that, in 1945, he enlisted in the Marines and was posted in the South Pacific, but returned without seeing action.

Sam's transformation from poetry-loving teen into professional soldier has provided lazy film critics with very rich pickings. Some speculate that he became a Marine to please his father, others reckon he did it because he didn't think the arts were a proper preoccupation for a grown man. Whatever the real reason, there's no denying that Sam was a man of contradiction. The thing is, and this is what the critics so often overlook, Peckinpah never made any attempt to disguise the different aspects of his personality. Read Sam's reviews and you'd think there was nothing to his pictures except blood hits and bitch slapping. Watch his movies and you see every single part of his person: the poet, the nihilist, the aesthete, the idealist, the sinner, the redeemer, the father, the lover, the fiend. Sam Peckinpah was a very able man but he wasn't able to hide his dichotomous nature from the general public. Then again, who's saying he wanted to disguise it in the first place?

Sam's contradictions didn't just affect the content of his films, they influenced the way in which he made movies. As a man who hated producers but loved making movies, Sam Peckinpah spent his entire life doing the thing he loved most with the people he liked least. Sam's spats with production executives really were in a league of their own. No one took such insane delight in torturing their superiors, or was willing to continue a fight even after a situation had been resolved. Sam Peckinpah may not lend himself well to single-word evaluation but he's very well suited to another of the lazy film journalist's devices, the list. Just check out the following catalogue of Sam's most colourful encounters with film folk.

1) The day *The Killer Elite* wrapped, Sam fired the following memo off to producer Arthur Lewis: "My problem is I do not suffer fools graciously and detest petty thievery and incompetence. Other than that I found you charming, and, on occasion, mildly entertaining." Peckinpah and Lewis never worked together again.

2) During the making of *The Cincinnati Kid*, Sam caused quite a stir by blind siding a member of the production staff called Frank Kowalski. It was a good job that Kowalski was one of Peckinpah's oldest friends or else Sam might have really hurt him.

3) Studios don't often allow directors to give interviews mid-shoot. This extract from an interview Sam gave to a German film magazine during the shooting of *Cross Of Iron* explains why: "I can't tell you what it's been like: delays, halts in shooting, no rushes, no film sometimes. The producer (Wolf C Hartwig) says it's trouble at the border. I asked him if not paying the crew was due to trouble at the border."

4) In 1970, having spent the last three years telling any journalist that would listen that producer Jerry Bresler's cuts had ruined his cavalry epic *Major Dundee*, Sam turned down an offer from Columbia to restore the picture, claiming that he was too busy shooting *The Ballad Of Cable Hogue*. As *Cable Hogue* editor Louis Lombardo recalled: "Sam realised the value of *Major Dundee* having been violated. It was something he could use against producers in years to come. If he had fixed it, it would have undermined his view that studios were heartless, artless institutions that were only interested in butchering a director's vision. By leaving it broke, he maintained the 'them-and-us' atmosphere that he thrived on."

5) During the American Film Institute's tribute to James Cagney in 1976, a well-oiled Sam stood up during a rambling speech by Jack Lemmon and bellowed: "We didn't come here to hear you talk about yourself! We came to honour Cagney! Get off the stage!" This outburst embarrassed many including producer Martin Baum

who had just finished making *The Killer Elite* with Sam and who was sat at the same table.

If Sam's rucks with producers were legendary, the list of films he never realised is also pretty impressive.

1) *My Pardner* - Sam fell in love with Max Evans' novel in 1970 when he was between studios. Unfortunately, he never re-established a strong enough foothold in Hollywood to get the picture made.

2) *The Hi-Lo Country* - Another Evans book which Peckinpah dragged from one major studio to another for the best part of 15 years (Sam also unsuccessfully pitched adaptations of Evans' *Castaway* and *One-Eyed Sky*). The book was eventually filmed by British director Stephen Frears in 1998 with Billy Crudup and Woody Harrelson in the leading roles. It was by no means a bad movie, but you imagine Sam, Warren Oates and James Coburn might have done a lot more with the material.

3) *Sometimes A Great Notion* - Although Sam could see many parallels between Ken Kesey's tale of an Oregon logging family and his own childhood experiences, he couldn't find anyone to bankroll a big-screen adaptation.

4) *Deliverance* - Peckinpah was perhaps the only person who could have improved on John Boorman's efforts, but he lost the gig when he quit Warner Brothers in 1970. As excellent as Burt Reynolds, Jon Voight, Ronny Cox and Ned Beatty are in Boorman's movie, you can't help thinking about what might have happened had Warren Oates, James Coburn, L Q Jones and John Chandler rowed off into the wilds with Uncle Sam at the tiller.

5) *The Shotgunners* - Shortly before he died, Peckinpah started work on a script with horror writer Stephen King. Entitled *The Shotgunners*, the screenplay centred on a band of villains who travel the country in a limousine, opening fire on any town they roll into. It was a slight idea, but with Sam and King attached, it was unlikely that it would have made for dull cinema. Sadly, Sam's involvement in the project was cut short by his untimely death.

To this catalogue of unmade films you could also add *Superman*, *Jeremiah Johnson*, *Summer Soldiers* and Dino de Laurentiis' remake of *King Kong*. As lists go it's quite a long one, but it's only slightly longer than the most important of all Peckinpah inventories: the list of Sam's classic pictures. The catalogue features the sort of films directors would sell their souls to shoot: *The Wild Bunch*, *Ride The High Country*, *Pat Garrett And Billy The Kid*, *Bring Me The Head Of Alfredo Garcia*, *Junior Bonner*, *Cross Of Iron*. Each and every one of them a masterpiece. Then there's the list of Sam's secondary pictures (*The Getaway*, *The Ballad Of Cable Hogue*, *Straw Dogs*, *Major Dundee*, *The Killer Elite*), which are pictures that most directors would consider unqualified triumphs.

Out of the 13 films Sam Peckinpah completed, at least 11 are of great merit, and upwards of 6 could be considered true classics. It's a measure of Sam's artistry that even his minor works, principally *The Deadly Companions*, have things to recommend them. So what is it about Peckinpah's movies that makes them so great? For the full, unexpurgated answer, you'll have to read the rest of this book. In short, and in this writer's opinion, the real key to Sam's films, the element that elevates them above your everyday Westerns and action movies, is the thing that a lot of critics like least about Sam's cinema: male camaraderie.

The key symbol of male togetherness in Peckinpah's pictures is the posse: the band of men brought together to perform a specific task. Posses, platoons, bunches and contingents are everywhere in Sam's cinema. For example, in *The Deadly Companions*, ex-cavalryman Yellowleg teams up with his arch rivals Turk and Billy to escort prostitute Kit across the desert together with the body of her dead son. Or *Ride The High Country*, where Steve Judd hires old friend Gil Westrum and young buck Heck Longtree to help him deliver money and pick up gold from a local mine. Or *Major Dundee* where one posse (a motley crew of Union soldiers, Confederate prisoners, black volunteers and assorted lowlife) hunts down another (a renegade band of Apache Indians) while being pursued by another (a contingent of French lancers). A similar conflict exists in *The Wild Bunch*, where Pike Bishop's soldiers of fortune do battle with railroad-sponsored bounty hunters, a US army unit *and* the massed forces of General Mapache. Posses also fight one another in *Pat Garrett And Billy The Kid* (William H Bonney's outfit are hunted to extinction by Garrett's allies), *Bring Me The Head Of Alfredo Garcia* (Garcia's family and El Jefe's henchmen take up arms to recover the bounty-friendly bonce), *The Killer Elite* (Mike Lockren's ComTeg agents fight George Hansen's splinter group and an army of ninjas), *Cross Of Iron* (Sergeant Steiner's platoon take on the German military elite *and* the entire Russian Army) and *Convoy* (truckers from 3 states band together to protest police corruption and poor working conditions).

And when he isn't singing the praises of the posse, Peckinpah is pointing up the dangers that await the man who faces the world alone. In *Junior Bonner*, the rodeo ace rides solo from one poorly-paid gig to another, waiting for extinction to catch up with him. Likewise, in *Bring Me The Head Of Alfredo Garcia*, Bennie perishes simply because he has no one to watch his back for him. Loners also fair badly in *Straw Dogs* (David Sumner loses his humanity when he responds to the merciless bullying of the village locals) and *Cross Of Iron* (the despicable Stransky alienates everybody and is left to fend off the advancing Russian hordes alone). The message in Sam's pictures would seem simple: work with others and survive, or work alone and die. It's an argument that's underpinned by the existence of so many double acts in the director's pictures (Gil and Steve in *High Country*, Pike & Dutch and Tector & Lyle in *The Wild Bunch*, Cable & Joshua and Taggart & Bowen in *The Ballad Of Cable Hogue*, Doc & Carol and Butler & Fran in *The Getaway*, Mike and Mac in *The Killer Elite*). In Peckinpah's world-view, working with another person is preferable to going solo.

(By way of a digression, Sam's passion for posses also coloured his life behind the camera. Look at the credits of Peckinpah's movies and you'll find the same names reappearing over and over again. On the acting front, Sam worked regularly with guys like Warren Oates, James Coburn, Dub Taylor, R G Armstrong, Jason Robards, L Q Jones, John Davis Chandler, Slim Pickens, Jack Dodson, Brian Keith, Chill Wills, Richard Bright, Bo Hopkins, Gig Young and Ben Johnson. Peckinpah also enjoyed long-standing relationships with editors Garth Craven, Roger Spottiswoode, Louis Lombardo and Robert Wolfe, cinematographers John

Coquillon and Lucien Ballard, composer Jerry Goldsmith and general assistants/good buddies Gordon Dawson, Frank Kowalski and Walter Kelley. All of the aforementioned could tell you that Sam Peckinpah wasn't an easy man to work for - he fired crew members the way Billy The Kid fired bullets. However, those who worked regularly with Sam knew that, if they gave him their all, he'd stand by them through anything. As L Q Jones put it: "If you gave Sam 100%, he treated you royally. If you gave him any less, he'd kick you from here to the gas station.")

Sadly, critics have never really praised this essential aspect of Sam's pictures. This is perhaps because Peckinpah's posses are synonymous with boorish behaviour (*The Wild Bunch* drink and fuck their way across Mexico, *Pat Garrett And Billy The Kid* are either seen with a bottle in their hand or a girl on their arm, etc.). But a more probable reason is that film critics, not being the most sociable of creatures, don't possess the emotional equipment needed to understand the importance of camaraderie. A lonely, 24/7 career, it's little wonder that writers don't play well with others. And since they operate alone, film writers will always struggle to understand why Sam Peckinpah made such a big deal about friendship.

Now, while I am a film writer (and a lazy film writer at that), I also play cricket and rugby union. And while I'm never going to raise The Ashes or The Webb-Ellis Cup, I've played enough of both sports to get a whiff of the camaraderie Sam considered worth capturing on camera. Of course, in Peckinpah's films, the friendship exists in the most extreme circumstances. (In *The Wild Bunch*, Pike's men know they have been painted into a corner. In *Pat Garrett*, Billy and his brother outlaws appreciate that their time is nearly up. In *Cross Of Iron*, the Germans realise it is only a matter of time before the Russians overpower them.) But even playing against Old Fullerians fourths on a wet, slate grey sky Saturday afternoon, you achieve some understanding of the importance of looking out for one another and sticking together. What's more, playing sports gives you some perspective on how a common cause can pull together the most disparate of bands - the rugby team I play for consists of hoteliers, mechanics, accountants, lorry drivers and factory workers.

Suggesting that rugby football is the key to understanding the films of Sam Peckinpah will no doubt amuse the film-writing community who probably assume that the only connection between the two entities are boorishness and misogyny. To see what I'm trying to get at here, check out an excellent video entitled *Living With Lions*. An account of the successful 1997 British Lions tour to South Africa, the cassette's many highlights include a speech that coach Ian McGeechan gave just prior to the second, decisive test. Trying to convince his side of the importance of the occasion, McGeechan explains that should they win today, in years to come, whenever the players meet they will exchange a certain look, a nod or a wink that will sum exactly what it meant to be part of a triumphant Lions side in South Africa. Now, I experience a variation on this look on the weekends when the Welwyn fifth team win. And the men in Sam Peckinpah's films also regularly exchange knowing glances. The only difference is that, while the looks I share are rather watered down, the smiles that, say, the members of *The Wild Bunch* swap are as powerful as they could possibly be for they are exchanged in the face of certain death.

And since I've mentioned misogyny, let's get something straight: Sam Peckinpah's films aren't misogynist. They're sexist, sure, but only in the way that all Westerns and action movies are. The problem is that there weren't too many care workers or recruitment consultants operating on the American prairie in the 1880s, so Sam can only show women performing their two principal frontier functions as housewives and as prostitutes. All the same, Peckinpah's films are considerably less sexist than modern Hollywood blockbusters in which women are portrayed as either helpless victims or ice pick-wielding dykes who achieve success only by adopting manly attitudes or by pandering to male fantasies.

Of course, Sam's alleged sexism is one of the reasons why there's still so much interest in his films. Controversy alone cannot account for the amazing hold Peckinpah has come to have over popular culture. Sam has had films dedicated to him (serial killer picture *Killer: A Journal Of Violence*). Collaborator and country-

and-western star Kris Kristofferson wrote a song about him. John Carpenter, Quentin Tarantino, Martin Scorsese, Paul Schrader, Walter Hill, George Miller, Ron Shelton, Paul Verhoeven, John Woo and Michael Bay are amongst the hundreds of directors who have sited Peckinpah as an influence upon their work. Primal Scream's *Vanishing Point* album featured a track called *If They Move... Kill 'Em*. At the height of their popularity, the Monty Python team performed a sketch called *Sam Peckinpah's Salad Days*, in which a tea-and -cucumber-sandwiches musical turns into a slow-motion bloodbath. Bristol trip hop legends Massive Attack were originally known as The Wild Bunch and continue to release records on a label of that name. The soundtrack to *Pat Garrett And Billy The Kid* provided the sample that returned soul singer Gabrielle to high estate. John Belushi's *Sam Peckinpah Directs...* was one of the comedian's finest contributions to *Saturday Night Live*. Steven Spielberg cribbed Sam's *Cross Of Iron* shooting strategies for the Oscar-winning *Saving Private Ryan*. And Sam fan Alex Cox's superb Mexican police movie *Highway Patrolman* was produced by a Japanese trading company called Cable Hogue. Add to this the countless Peckinpah biographies and documentaries and the excitement that greeted the recent release of the director's cuts of *The Wild Bunch* and *Pat Garrett And Billy The Kid* and you really wouldn't think that Sam Peckinpah died in 1985.

Although he punched like an irate kangaroo, drank like a thirsty pike and snorted like an asthmatic pig, it's for his films that Sam Peckinpah will ultimately be remembered. Great films. Amazing films. Films that, in my opinion, provide cinema's most accurate representation of the balance of life. Going back to the misogyny debate, anyone who takes umbrage at the way women are depicted in Sam's movies ought to look at the way the director portrays men: cowardly, vain, boastful, thug-like, boorish, psychotic, bloodthirsty. Blokes don't come out of Sam's films at all well. Indeed, when it comes to the human condition, Peckinpah sees an awful lot of misery, pain and misfortune. Like the night's sky, this bleak, black canvas, is peppered with minute flashes of light: brief moments of joy, compassion, redemption and tenderness. They're not much, but they're the reason we in the real world keep on living and they're sufficient to convince Sam's desperadoes that life is worth fighting for to the bitter end.

Sam Peckinpah: fearless coward, pugilist poet, sane mad man, gregarious loner, pessimistic optimist, one of the best reasons ever for going to the movies and a film-maker who can only really be described as 'bloody' if the word precedes 'magnificent.'

Don Siegel

Sam Peckinpah is the only man in history to go from serving in the United States Marine Corps to working as a stagehand on the *Liberace TV Hour*. It was as a production assistant at KLAC-TV that Sam discovered what he wanted to do with the rest of his life.

Peckinpah's early television duties included sweeping stages, moving sets and helping actors rehearse their lines. The work wasn't well paid but it let Sam see every aspect of the production process. After months of watching what researchers, producers and writers contributed to the shows, Sam decided that what he wanted to do was direct. He got his first gig in 1953, shooting a production of Tennessee Williams' *Portrait Of A Madonna*, starring Sam's then-wife Marie Selland. The end product was so naive and stagy Peckinpah received just one other directing assignment during his time with KLAC, a considerably less ambitious 10-minute children's TV show called *Tom Tit Tot*.

As *Portrait Of A Madonna* proved to Peckinpah's superiors that he didn't yet have what it took to direct, it proved to Sam that directing was the only thing he wanted to do. His search for more behind-the-camera experience and a better wage brought him to Hollywood's Poverty Row. Now known the world over as the creator of *Coogan's Bluff*, *Dirty Harry* and *The Shootist*, Don Siegel was making B-pictures when Sam Peckinpah paid him a call in 1954. Remembering the meeting in his excellent autobiography *A Siegel Film*, the great man writes: "I liked Sam's wit, charm and ambition. I told him I had never had a 'gopher' before. 'What's a gopher, Sir?' 'Oh someone who 'goes for' anything and everything: coffee, paper clips, girls... you name it!" And so for 3 years, under the job title of 'dialogue director,' and occasionally credited as David Peckinpah, Sam served as Don Siegel's gopher on *Riot In*

Cell Block 11, *Private Hell 36*, *Annapolis Story*, *Invasion Of The Bodysnatchers* and *Crime In The Streets*. Sam's coups during this time included performing an uncredited rewrite on *Bodysnatchers*, a film in which he also had a small role, and using his legal connections to win over the governor of the prison used during the shooting of *Riot In Cell Block 11*. In between his stints with Siegel, Sam worked as a dialogue director with Charles Marquis on *Seven Angry Men* (1955) and the great Jacques Tourneur on *Wichita* (1955), in which he had also a small part as a pilot, and *Great Day In The Morning* (1956).

It's perhaps because of their close association that critics often talk of Siegel and Peckinpah's pictures sharing certain thematic concerns. I can't see it myself. While Siegel was obsessed with loners (to wit: *The Killers*, *Dirty Harry*, *Charley Varrick*), Peckinpah was convinced of the positive affects of male camaraderie. This isn't to say there aren't similarities between the two men's work. On the contrary, their films prove that they are both highly accomplished at handling actors and action sequences. These, however, are artistic similarities. As far as codas are concerned, the two couldn't have been more different.

If the notion that Sam and Don shared a philosophy is ill-founded, there can be no doubting the pair's close friendship. Peckinpah never forgot the opportunity that Siegel had given him and warmly referred to Don as 'his patron' in interviews. And years later, when Sam couldn't even get work waiting tables, Siegel proved just how good a mate he was by asking Peckinpah to head up the second unit on the Bette Midler action comedy *Jinxed!*

The Television Years

Sam Peckinpah returned to television in 1955 to work as a writer and director. Besides 11 episodes of *Gunsmoke* ('The Queue'which was Sam's first script sale, 'Yorky,' 'The Guitar,' 'Cooter,' 'How To Die For Nothing,' 'The Roundup,' 'Legal Revenge,' 'Poor Pearl,' 'Jealousy,' 'Dirt,' 'How To Kill A Woman'), he penned instalments of *20th Century Fox Hour* ('End Of A Gun,' for which he received a Writers Guild Of America nomination for Best Western), *Klondike* ('Klondike Fever,' 'Swoger's Mill,' 'Man Without A Gun,' 'The

Kidder'), *Boots And Saddles* ('The Captain'), *Tales Of Wells Fargo* ('Apache Gold'), *Tombstone Territory* ('Johnny Ringo's Last Ride'), *Trackdown* ('The Town'), *Have Gun - Will Travel, The Singer* and *Pony Express*. It was as a director and producer that Sam was to score his greatest TV success. His contributions to *Broken Arrow* (for which Sam wrote the episodes 'The Teacher,' 'The Knife Fighter,' 'The Assassin' and wrote and directed 'The Transfer'), *Zane Grey Theater* ('Miss Jenny,' 'Lonesome Road'), *Route 66* ('Mon Petite Chow') and *Dick Powell Theater* ('Pericles On 31st Street,' 'The Losers') showed his fellow small-screen directors up for the talentless hacks they were.

The Western series Sam created were also streets ahead of the standard TV fare. *The Rifleman*, which Peckinpah produced with Arnold Laven, detailed the adventures of hired gun Lucas McCain and his young son, Mark. Sam once said that the series was the 'story of a boy who grows to manhood learning what it's all about,' although it is *The Rifleman*'s other plot strand, about McCain's efforts to escape his violent past, that perhaps held the greater appeal for Peckinpah. As originally conceived by Sam, the series was deeply autobiographical (Dunlap, the property McCain buys, shares its name with Peckinpah's grandparents' ranch) and extremely seedy: the 'Boarding House' episode, with its pimps, drunks and prostitutes, would appear incredibly dark to anyone whose idea of a 50s TV Western was *Champion The Wonder Horse*. Unfortunately, the positive reaction to Peckinpah's pitch in the boardroom led 2 other execs to glom their names to the production. It was the involvement of these execs that subverted the concept of the show, which in turn led Sam to quit *The Rifleman* after just 6 episodes ('The Sharpshooter,' 'Home Ranch,' 'The Marshal,' 'The Money Gun,' 'The Baby-sitter,' 'The Boarding House').

The frustration over what had happened with *The Rifleman*, together with a general dissatisfaction with the quality of TV Westerns, led Sam to produce a second series, *The Westerner*. "I created the show," Peckinpah said, "because of anger at never-miss sheriffs, always-right marshals, whitewashed gunfighters - the mistakeless 'redwoods' who dominate the Western field today." Sam further stated that *The Westerner*'s protagonist Dave Blassingame was "unlettered (most of these guys couldn't read or write), not too bright, certainly unheroic. No hero, no lawman, no bounty hunter: a real saddle tramp." Jam-packed with Peckinpah posturing and featuring a superb turn from Brian Keith, *The Westerner* was a superior TV entertainment, but since it didn't do what commercial television programmes are meant to do, principally shift huge quantities of soap, Coca-Cola and dog food, its tenure was brief.

By the time *The Westerner* came off air, Sam Peckinpah had considerably bigger fish to fry...

On The Hoof

Sam Peckinpah's career in motion pictures got off to something of a false start when, in 1961, he was hired to write and direct a Western by Marlon Brando but was fired after turning in the first draft. Based on Charles Neider's novel *The Authentic Death Of Hendry Jones*, *One Eyed Jacks* was a fictionalised account of lawman Pat Garrett's pursuit of Billy The Kid. It was a picture Sam seemed born to make. After spending 6 months on the screenplay, Peckinpah received a call from Brando telling him that Stanley Kubrick would now direct. Much as Sam regretted losing the gig, his dismissal was probably for the best as it was unlikely that he would have been able to work with Brando, a man whose policy of banging a gong during production meetings so annoyed Kubrick, he left the lardy method genius to shoot the film himself.

Sam didn't receive a screen credit for his work on *One Eyed Jacks* but he retained the rights to his version of the script and was able to paste some of the meatier scenes into his later pictures. What's more, Peckinpah's association with Brando's Pennebaker productions, together with his TV work, had caught the attention the leading Hollywood studios. His first proper gig in motion pictures was just a few short months away...

The Deadly Companions (1961)

Cast: Maureen O'Hara (Kit Tilden), Brian Keith (Yellowleg), Steve Cochran (Billy), Chill Wills (Turk), Strother Martin (Parson), Will Wright (Doctor), Jim O'Hara (Cal), Peter O'Crotty (Mayor), Billy Vaughan (Mead), Robert Sheldon (Gambler), John Hamilton (Gambler), Hank Gobble (Bartender), Buck Sharpe (Indian)

Crew: Director Sam Peckinpah, Writers A S Fleischman & Charles B FitzSimons (uncredited), Producer Charles B FitzSimons, Music Marlin Skiles & Charles B FitzSimons, Cinematographer William H Clothier, Editor Stanley E Rabjohn, Production Manager Lee Lukather, Costume Designers Frank Beetson Snr & Sheila O'Brien

Also Known As: Trigger Happy

Story: It's the late 1860s and former Union Sergeant Yellowleg is hot on the trail of Turk, the Confederate deserter who tried to scalp him 7 years earlier at Chickamauga. Yellowleg finally finds his quarry holed up in a bar but instead of doing away with him, he persuades Turk and his partner Billy to join him on a bank raid.

On arriving at Gila City, Arizona, the trio find another band of outlaws in town to turn over the same establishment. A gun battle breaks out during which an old war wound leads to Yellowleg accidentally shooting the son of Kit Tilden, a local prostitute. The grief-stricken Tilden wants to bury her son next to the body of her late husband in Serengo, a ghost town many miles away. Out of guilt, Yellowleg offers to ride with her across the Indian-infested desert. He coerces Turk and Billy into riding with them only for the latter to try and rape Tilden.

After Turk and Billy dessert, Yellowleg and Tilden ride on alone to Serengo to bury the boy. Once the deed is done, the duo are rejoined by Turk and Billy who have just robbed the Gila City bank. Yellowleg, who is slowly falling in love with Tilden, is desperate to kill Turk but his war injury prevents him from doing so. Instead, Billy shoots Turk but fails to kill him, allowing the old man to kill his partner before being dragged back to Gila City to face the music. Tilden and Yellowleg, meanwhile, ride off into the sunset, the former having apparently come to terms with the latter having murdered her son.

Subtext: The Deadly Companions dates back to a time when, instead of subtexts, Westerns made do with nice hats, lots of horses and dialogue such as, "some of you stay here and guard the girl. We'll cut them off at the pass."

Themes & Ideas: As we'll soon see, Sam Peckinpah had relatively little say over the content of *The Deadly Companions*. Nevertheless, the film contains themes (e.g., betrayal, revenge, redemption, the lot of the fighting man) that Sam would examine and re-examine throughout his film career. Were this really a Peckinpah Western, however, there'd be less attention paid to Tilden and Yellowleg's unlikely romance and a whole lot more said about how you prevent a corpse from decomposing on a trek across the desert. (Sam would eventually get to address the practicalities of this matter in *Bring Me The Head Of Alfredo Garcia*).

Backstory: Sam was hired to shoot *The Deadly Companions* at the suggestion of Brian Keith who had starred as Dave Blassingame in *The Westerner*. Producer Charles B FitzSimons refused Sam permission to rewrite the so-so script. What's more, FitzSimons stood next to Peckinpah throughout the shoot, telling him how to set up every shot and preventing him from giving direction to Maureen O'Hara, FitzSimons' sister. Then, once the shoot was over, Peckinpah was locked out of the editing suite.

Peckinpah's Posse: Like John Ford, Sam Peckinpah worked with a stock company of actors and technicians. He started assembling his army of allies while he was still working in television and a number of these friends appeared in his debut feature. Besides Keith, both Chill Wills and Steve Cochran had worked on Peckinpah's TV Westerns. *The Deadly Companions* also features Strother Martin who would become as much a part of Sam's cinema as shotguns and slow motion.

Legacy: After the film was released, A S Fleischman published *The Deadly Companions* as a novel. Alas, it is no longer in print.

Verdict: Clichéd, predictable, boring, *The Deadly Companions* is everything Peckinpah's other Westerns aren't. Still, judging from the problems he had making the movie, Sam wasn't really to blame for the film's failure and, besides, there have been more inauspicious debuts. 2/5

Ride The High Country (1962)

Cast: Joel McCrea (Steve Judd), Randolph Scott (Gil Westrum), Mariette Hartley (Elsa Knudsen), Ron Starr (Heck Longtree), Edgar Buchanan (Judge Tolliver), R G Armstrong (Joshua Knudsen), Jenie Jackson (Kate), James Drury (Billy Hammond), L Q Jones (Sylvus Hammond), Warren Oates (Henry Hammond), John Anderson (Elder Hammond), John Davis Chandler (Jimmy Hammond), Carmen Phillips (Saloon Girl)

Crew: Director Sam Peckinpah, Writers N B Stone Jnr & Sam Peckinpah (uncredited) & William S Roberts (uncredited), Music George Bassman, Cinematographer Lucien Ballard, Editor Frank Santillo, Art Directors George W Davis & Leroy Coleman, Set Decoration Henry Grace & Otto Siegel, Assistant Director Hal Polaire

UK Title: Guns In The Afternoon

Story: Ageing lawman Steve Judd is contracted by the bankers of Starbuck to travel to Coarsegold, a mining town where the prospectors want to exchange their hoards for hard currency. Aware of the dangers of such a journey, Judd hires the services of old friend turned carnival performer Gil Westrum and young buck Heck Longtree. As they set off for the mountains, Judd is unaware that his partners plan to rob him on the return journey.

On the out journey, the posse take shelter at the house of God-fearing farmer Joshua Knudsen. Longtree is smitten with Joshua's daughter, Elsa, who tells him that her fiancé, Billy Hammond, is a prospector in Coarsegold. The next morning when the trio resume their journey, Elsa tags along, determined to escape her wrathful father and marry her Billy.

On arriving in Coarsegold, Judd and Westrum get down to business while Elsa seeks out her sweetheart, much to the chagrin of the love-struck Longtree. However, Billy Hammond is not a decent, honourable man. Rather he is a brutish, lascivious thug, every bit as detestable as his 4 inbred brothers.

A wedding is hastily arranged and at a service held in the town's whorehouse, Elsa and Billy are declared man and wife. When 2 of Billy's brothers try to rape his new bride, Judd and Westrum intervene. The next morning, Westrum confronts the Judge who conducted the ceremony and tells him to lie about owning a marriage license. To the Hammonds' chagrin, the posse are allowed to ride away, taking Elsa and the gold with them.

Heading for home, Westrum and Longtree try and fail to hold up Judd who is way too smart for the ageing carny and the naive cowboy. Before the lawman can resolve the situation, the quartet are ambushed by the Hammonds who have found out that the wedding was legal after all. They demand to have Elsa back but are sent packing by Judd together with Longtree, who has realised the error of his ways.

Before they return home, the posse ride to the Knudsen farm to return Elsa to her father, only to find that the Hammonds have got there before them. The brothers have murdered Joshua Knudsen and will kill the trio unless they hand over the girl. Guns are drawn and Longtree is shot and wounded, leaving the old duo of Judd and Westrum to go head-to-head with the villainous brothers. In the final shoot-out, the Hammonds bite the bullet but Judd is also fatally wounded. The reformed Westrum informs his dying friend that the gold will be safely returned. He, Longtree and Elsa then ride away, leaving Judd to look one last time at the mountains he once ruled.

Subtext: Judd's icy relationship with the bankers parallels Peckinpah's awful experiences with producers (Sam: "Money's what it's all about. I'm dealing with a product that costs several million dollars. When you are dealing in millions, you're dealing with people at their meanest."). The film also has a distinct autobiographical quality, with the towns and villages being named after places Peckinpah grew up in and the dialogue coming straight from the mouth of Sam's dad. As Peckinpah once recalled: "'I want to enter my house justified' is my father's. We talked about that just before he died." Sadly, David Peckinpah Snr didn't live to see the release of his son's second film.

Themes & Ideas: Real men ride together (Judd's trio and the Hammond clan are classic good and bad guy posses, respectively), friendship is a higher value that shouldn't be betrayed but often is (Judd is overturned by his old friend Westrum), the times they are a-changing (the film begins with a camel defeating a horse in a race and with Judd almost being run down by a motorcar), money men are bad! (the bankers are officious little men), religious folk are absolutely barking (Bible-thumping farmer Joshua Knudsen is completely tonto. Be sure to check out the whore-fixated epitaph engraved on his wife's tombstone), deathbed scenes are super (Judd's swansong is right up there with Rutger Hauer's 'tears in rain' *Blade Runner* farewell in the list of classic screen goodbyes), a man's best friend is his gun (scrapping comes as second nature to Judd, Westrum and the Hammond boys), male camaraderie is a good thing (the brothers Hammond may be a lice-infested band of murdering rapists but, boy, do they love each other), ultra-violence (the film's gentle, strolling manner doesn't prepare you in the slightest for the grisly discovery of Joshua Knudsen's body), redemption is available to all (Longtree and Westrum restore Judd's original faith in them).

Backstory: Peckinpah spent the entire film at war with the execs. Then, when he screened the picture to the studio heads, they took one look at the whorehouse footage and dumped the film on the bottom half of a double bill. Given the autobiographical nature of the work, it's not hard to imagine how much this must have hurt Peckinpah. It was only *High Country*'s remarkable reviews that saved Sam from a swift return to television.

Peckinpah's Posse: Ride The High Country united Sam with Warren Oates, who had starred in 'The Marshal' episode of *The Rifleman* and saw both L Q Jones and John Davis Chandler inducted into Peckinpah's peculiar big-screen family. This was also the first film in which R G Armstrong played a jumbo barmy Bible-spouter for 'Bloody Sam.' On the technical side, Lucien Ballard's impressive work guaranteed him gigs with Peckinpah for several years to come.

A Posse Member Speaks: Actor L Q Jones: "If Sam had never made another movie after *Ride The High Country*, people would still be talking about it as one of *the* great Westerns. Because Sam made 4 or 5 other outstanding Westerns, *High Country* has sort of been forgotten. Make no mistake about it, though: *Ride The High Country* is right up there with *The Wild Bunch* and *Pat Garrett And Billy The Kid*. When we were making it, we knew we were creating a movie that was going to last. Us Hammond brothers, Warren, John and I, kept looking at each other and grinning, because we knew what we were making was something really special."

Straight From The Horseman's Mouth: i) Judd: "I just want to enter my house justified." ii) Westrum: "Don't worry about anything. I'll take care of it, just like you would have." Judd: "Hell, I know that. I always did. You just forgot it for a while, that's all."

Verdict: Although it superficially resembles the standard horse operas of its age, this is a remarkable, genre-redefining work, brimming over with the sort of complex morality you seldom find in PG certificate movies. McCrea and Scott are excellent and the film gives them the send-off they deserve (neither worked in movies again), but the real star here is Peckinpah, whose determination to prove how the West was lost is matched by his appreciation of pace and good set pieces. Some have called it a bloodless *Wild Bunch*, but that suggests *Ride The High Country* lacks power. It doesn't, it's just a little short on red stuff. 5/5

Major Dundee (1965)

Cast: Charlton Heston (Major Amos Dundee), Richard Harris (Captain Benjamin Tyreen), James Coburn (Samuel Potts), Jim Hutton (Lieutenant Graham), Michael Anderson Jnr (Tim Ryan), Senta Berger (Teresa Santiago), Mario Adorf (Sergeant Gomez), Brock Peters (Aesop), Warren Oates (O W Hadley), Ben Johnson (Sergeant Chillum), R G Armstrong (Reverend Dahlstrom), L Q Jones (Arthur Hadley), Slim Pickens (Wiley), Karl Swenson (Captain Walker), Michael Pate (Sierra Charriba), John Davis Chandler (Jimmy Lee Benteen), Dub Taylor (Priam), Albert Carrier (Captain Jacques Tremaine), Jose Carlos Ruiz (Riago), Aurora Clavel (Melinche), Begonia Palacios (Linda), Enrique Lucero (Dr Aguillar), Francisco Reyguera (Old Apache)

Crew: Director Sam Peckinpah, Writers Harry Julian Fink & Oscar Saul & Sam Peckinpah, Story Harry Julian Fink, Producer Jerry Bresler, Assistant Producer Rick Rosenberg, Music Daniele Amfitheatrof, Cinematographer Lucien Ballard, Editors William A Lyon & Don Starling & Howard Kunin, Art Director Al Ybarra,

Production Manager Francisco Day, Assistant Directors Floyd Joyer & John Veitch

Story: 1865 and renegade Apache Sierra Charriba and his band of warriors rule the roost over an area 3 times the size of Texas. A particularly vicious attack on a ranch house incurs the wrath of Union Major Amos Dundee, a decorated war hero who has been left guarding a prison full of captured Confederates after conducting his own war at Gettysburg. Such is Dundee's determination to pursue the Apache, he supplements his meagre forces with a band of black volunteers and a contingent of POWs, the latter under Captain Benjamin Tyreen, an Irish nobleman who was good friends with Dundee at West Point until the latter testified against him at his court martial.

A night time Apache ambush leaves Dundee's men in disarray and they decide to rest up at a local village. After seeing off a band of French servicemen, the Major's men settle down to some serious merrymaking while he romances Teresa, an Austrian nurse. When the impromptu fiesta is over, the posse resume their quest only to be held up yet again when Dundee receives a leg wound. Matters are further complicated by the execution of one of the Confederates, O W Hadley, for desertion.

Eventually, Dundee's men get going again and they confront and kill Sierra Charriba and his tribesmen. With the Indian slain, Tyreen challenges Dundee to a duel. Before blows can be exchanged, a contingent of French lancers ride into view. In an epic riverside confrontation, Tyreen sacrifices himself to allow Dundee and his battered brigade to ride home to Texas and safety.

Subtext: Major Dundee superficially seems to have a lot to say about national and racial identity. The Union versus The Confederacy, the new world Dundee versus the old world Tyreen, black versus white, white man versus red, everybody versus the French. It's good, meaty stuff, or rather it would be were not the points Peckinpah wanted to make muffled by the producer Jerry Bresler's unwarranted cuts. Still, the image of arch-Confederate Tyreen rallying the troops around the Union flag before riding into certain death is one that lingers in the memory.

Themes & Ideas: Mirrors (when he is in the hospital, Dundee gives himself a thorough examination. He doesn't like what he sees), fast cutting and slow motion (the film hints at the montage effects that Peckinpah would perfect in *The Wild Bunch*), real men ride together (*Major Dundee* is packed full of bands, posses, legions, brigades and contingents. Hadley's execution is a warning to those who abandon their comrades), ultra-violence (Tyreen is hacked to pieces in the final scene), a man's best friend is his gun (Everybody in *Major Dundee* is itching for a fight; Tyreen wants to kill Dundee, Dundee wants the head of Sierra Charriba and everybody wants a piece of the French), the law is an ass (Dundee and Tyreen are both murderers, the only difference being that Dundee has restricted his killing to the field of battle), the times they are a-changing (the black characters are articulate, intelligent men and not your typical happy-go-lucky, all singin', all dancin' ex-slaves. Mexico is in the hands of the French), religious folk are barking mad (Reverend Dahlstrom isn't as extreme as *High Country*'s Joshua Knudsen but he's still no Derek Nimmo), male camaraderie is a positive thing (the fiesta brings Dundee's disparate band together), women are trouble (it's while Dundee is romancing Teresa that he gets shot by the Apache), revenge is bittersweet (although Dundee completes his quest, there is no sense of achievement or release), redemption is available to all (Tyreen begins the film a prisoner on a murder charge and ends it a war hero) but not everybody wants to take it (Dundee seems to think he deserves the bad things that have and will happen to him. He is the embodiment of Peckinpah's belief that shit sometimes happens because people want it to. Even though he fulfils his quest, he ends the movie the same bitter, broken man), at the end the protagonists ride off into the sunset albeit it in atypical fashion (Dundee's platoon leave the field of battle every bit as battered as the defeated French).

Backstory: The film that nearly ended Sam's career, *Major Dundee* almost fell apart before it began. Although he was delighted to get a shot at big-budget film-making, Peckinpah hated the original Harry Julien Fink (*Dirty Harry*) script and insisted on rewriting it. This didn't please Jerry Bresler, the producer who had got the project green lit and who saw no reason to tamper with the Fink screenplay.

The fights Peckinpah and Bresler had over the script were nothing compared to what happened once the production moved to Mexico. Bresler, who didn't understand why the film couldn't be shot on Columbia's back lot, was enraged by Sam's on and off-screen excesses and fired off endless memos to the studio, detailing the money and time Peckinpah was 'wasting.'

Rather than sacking Sam mid-production, the Columbia chiefs waited until he had finished shooting the picture and then barred him from the editing. It was a tactic that incensed Peckinpah who launched a savage attack on the studio in the film press. His reward for this outburst was a place on Hollywood's infamous blacklist. It would be 4 years before he directed another feature film.

Peckinpah's Posse: Oates, Jones and Chandler are all back on board as are Ballard and Armstrong. Amongst those earning their stripes are Ben Johnson, Dub Taylor, Slim Pickens and James Coburn.

A Posse Member Speaks: Actor L Q Jones: "*Major Dundee* was a really hard shoot. There was a real feeling throughout our whole time in Mexico that all of our hard work was being undone by the producers back in Hollywood. Of course, all the studio interference didn't make Sam the easiest person to be around.

"Sam tried to drag Heston to the local brothels, but Charlton wasn't interested so he'd sit outside while Sam went in and did his stuff. Of course, *Major Dundee* is famous as the film where Charlton Heston tried to run down Sam with his horse. But it wasn't really an unhappy film as far as relationships between the cast and crew were concerned. Charlton really respected Sam as an artist; he understood what Sam was hoping to achieve. And while I think Sam thought Chuck was a bit of a stuffed shirt, he told me that he was delighted with his performance as Dundee. No, our problems were with the producers.

"Everyone got sick. Warren Oates was so ill we thought he was going to have to be sent home. Me and John Chandler weren't too good either. We weren't a healthy bunch of people to be around.

"Then, when we got home, we discovered that we were right all along and the studio had been dismantling the movie even as we were making it. It was the studio that lost out, though. Sam had other great films in him. If they'd only let him get on with it, he'd have made a great film for them, too. *Major Dundee* still is pretty amazing, but if Sam had been left alone, it would have been a classic."

Straight From The Horseman's Mouth: i) Tyreen: "Until the Apache is taken or destroyed." ii) Ryan: "He (Sierra Charriba) looks so small now." Dundee: "He was big enough, son." iii) Dundee: "By midnight tonight, I want every man in this platoon drunker than a fiddler's bitch."

Verdict: This is a film you'd love to like more than you actually can. Conceived by Peckinpah as "*Moby Dick* on horseback," a poorly-edited script and colossal studio interference turned this into a shaggy old mammoth of a movie - woolly in places, awe-inspiring in others. At its best (the relationship between Dundee and Tyreen, O W Hadley's execution scene, the charge of the French lancers), it rivals anything in the Peckinpah canon. It's just a shame that the picture got lumbered with a love story it doesn't require and some lamentably improbable plotting. A botched masterpiece then, but given the current fashion for director's cuts and re-releases we may yet get to see the same unexpurgated 154-minute cut that Richard Harris described as the greatest film he ever appeared in. 3/5

Ride Lonesome

Being blacklisted by Jerry Bresler might not have hurt Sam's career too much had he not screwed up his next directing gig so badly. Signed up by MGM the moment he was dropped by Columbia, Peckinpah looked set to score the first hit of his career when he was assigned to *The Cincinnati Kid*. Richard Jessup's best-selling gambling novel had been transformed into a vehicle for hot property Steve McQueen. All Sam had to do was show up on set every day, say 'action,' 'cut' and 'print' and by the end of shooting, his career would be back on track. Like many a sure thing before it, *The Cincinnati Kid* almost didn't make it out of the starting gate.

McQueen's co-star Spencer Tracy quit, the combined talents of Paddy Chayefsky (*Network*), Ring Lardner Jnr (*M*A*S*H*) and Frank D Gilroy (*The Only Game In Town*) couldn't lick the screenplay and Peckinpah fell out with producer Martin Ranshoff. The first 2 problems were taken care of by the hiring of Edward G Robinson and Terry Southern. The third was overcome by the firing of Sam Peckinpah.

To upset one major studio may be considered a misfortune. To upset 2 makes you look like a bit of an arsehole. Out of favour as a director, Peckinpah tried to find work as a writer. He dusted down his first feature-length screenplay *The Glory Guys*, and sold it to *Rifleman* co-creator Arnold Laven. Sam was also hired to write and direct *Villa Rides* for Yul Brynner, but was fired after the star read the first draft. "Brynner said I didn't understand Mexico," Peckinpah told reporters. This is like saying Lassie didn't understand barking.

In the end, it was Sam's old stomping ground, television, that paved the way for his return to motion pictures. Summoned to a meeting at ABC, Peckinpah was asked if he'd like to write and direct a TV movie based on Katherine Anne Porter's novella *Noon Wine*. Since Sam couldn't even find work directing traffic, he signed the contract there and then.

Peckinpah seized the opportunity to repair his reputation with both hands. His tireless work resulted in nominations for Best Television Adaptation from The Writers Guild Of America and Best Television Direction from The Directors Guild of America. On its completion, Peckinpah described *Noon Wine* as his favourite film, but he's said that about virtually all of his movies at one time or another. Whatever its merits, *Noon Wine* made Sam hireable again. After proving the film wasn't a fluke with a second successful TV job (an episode of *Bob Hope's Chrysler Theater*, 'That Lady Is My Wife'), he got a telephone call from Warner Brothers...

Back In The Saddle

As the films he made between 1969 and 1974 illustrate, Sam Peckinpah didn't waste his second shot at the big time.

The Wild Bunch (1969)

Cast: William Holden (Pike Bishop), Ernest Borgnine (Dutch Engstrom), Robert Ryan (Deke Thornton), Edmond O'Brien (Old Sykes), Warren Oates (Lyle Gorch), Ben Johnson (Tector Gorch), Jaime Sanchez (Angel), Emilio Fernandez (Mapache), Strother Martin (Coffer), L Q Jones (T C), Albert Dekker (Pat Harrigan), Bo Hopkins (Crazy Lee), Dub Taylor (Mayor Wainscoat), Jorge Russek (Zamorra), Alfonso Arau (Herrera), Chano Urueta (Don Jose), Sonia Amelio (Teresa), Aurora Clavel (Aurora), Elsa Cardenas (Elsa), Fernando Wagner (German Army Officer)

Crew: Director Sam Peckinpah, Writers Walon Green & Sam Peckinpah, Story Walon Green & Roy N Sickner, Producer Phil Feldman, Associate Producer Roy N Sickner, Music Jerry Fielding, Cinematographer Lucien Ballard, Editors Louis Lombardo & Robert L Wolfe (associate), Art Director Edward Carrere, Costume Designer Gordon Dawson, Production Manager William Faralla, Assistant Directors Cliff Coleman & Fred Gammon

Story: Morning. A high street. A group of children throw scorpions onto an anthill and watch the insects writhe. A temperance group parade through the town, extolling the virtues of the dry life. A platoon of soldiers ride into town and approach the post office. Only these aren't real soldiers, they're The Wild Bunch, the most low-down posse of bandidos that ever walked this side of the Rio Grande.

Assembled by the ageing Pike Bishop to pull off an ambitious bank robbery, the Bunch are about to make off with the loot when they're ambushed by a group of bounty hunters led by Deke Thornton, an old friend of Bishop's who has been press-ganged into working for the railroads. During the carnage that ensues, Bishop and 5 of his affiliates ride to safety while the street runs heavy with the blood of the remaining members of the Bunch, several of the bounty hunters and a hell of a lot of townsfolk.

At their rendezvous, the surviving Bunch members - Bishop, Dutch, Angel, Sykes and Lyle and Tector Gorch - discover that the bags of money they lifted are in fact filled with washers. For a moment, it looks as if the group might implode but instead they decide to travel south to Mexico to hole up in Angel's home village. There, they enjoy a fiesta that is spoilt only by the news that Angel's sweetheart Teresa has been kidnapped by the villainous General Mapache.

Determined to rescue the girl, the Bunch ride to Mapache's encampment where they discover Teresa in the arms of the fat, oily warlord. In a moment of madness, Angel kills his girlfriend, an action that looks certain to get the Bunch killed until Bishop offers to hijack a train full of guns that Mapache has had his eyes on.

Guns aren't the only thing the train is carrying. Thornton is also along for the ride as are the surviving bounty killers and a small squadron of soldiers. Even with all this firepower, the ex-Bunch member is unable to prevent Bishop from riding off with the guns, a box of which Angel gives to his townsfolk to help them in their fight against Mapache.

Delighted with his new weapons, Mapache is less pleased to hear of Angel's misdoing and tortures the young Mexican by tying him to the back of his motorcar. Although they briefly return to their old drinking and whoring ways, Bishop and the rest of the Bunch realise that it would be wrong to abandon their compadre. So they walk the length of the town for a final showdown with Mapache and his blood-hungry horde. In the struggle that follows, virtually the entire village perish alongside Lyle, Tector, Bishop, Angel and Dutch.

As dusk falls, Deke Thornton rides into town where he is confronted by an almost apocalyptic sight. Leaving the bounty hunters to pick over the bodies with the rest of the vultures, Thornton looks for the remains of his former friends. With the corpses picked clean, the bounty killers are ambushed by Angel's townsfolk and Thornton is left together with the bunch's one surviving member, Sykes, to ride off in search of fresh adventure.

Subtext: Alex Cox mentioned on the BBC's *Moviedrome* that *The Wild Bunch*, "with its random cruelty, its senseless massacres, high-tech killing and gangsters dressed as US soldiers taking hostages and murdering old ladies, feels like an early film about the Vietnam War." Peckinpah had very grave concerns about 'Nam (he sent a telegram to Nixon to protest the pardoning of Lieutenant William Calley, the man who orchestrated the My Lai Massacre). Although it might comment on the United States' foreign policy at that time, *The Wild Bunch* is considerably more concerned with the notions of men out of time and the end of days. (Incidentally, Alex Cox is better qualified than most to talk about US counter-insurgency and the cinema of Sam Peckinpah. Made in 1987, Cox's *Walker* used the true story of a 19th century American businessman who made himself president of Nicaragua to comment upon the Reagan administration's interference in Central American affairs. Quirky and compelling, *Walker* was written by Rudolph Wurlitzer, aka the author of Sam's *Pat Garrett And Billy The Kid*, and the picture does have a distinct Peckinpah feel about it, as do Cox's spoof Western *Straight To Hell* and his superior police picture, *Highway Patrolman*.)

Themes & Ideas: Fast cutting and slow motion (Peckinpah had experimented with this technique before but here editors Louis Lombardo and Robert Wolfe combine slow motion and live action perfectly. The film contains 3,643 cuts, more than in any other Technicolor film), mirrors (Pike's death is hastened by his shooting the reflection of a pistol-packin' whore rather than the whore herself. Also, when Pike is with the young prostitute, prior to the final assault on Mapache, her youth and innocence mirror his age, shame and debauchery), ultra-violence (when Peckinpah originally shot the slashing of Angel's throat, a fault in the mechanism led to the blood shooting a full twenty metres. The take Sam ended up with is still pretty strong stuff), kids are lil' bastards (the children at the beginning of the movie torture scorpions. A small boy fires the bullet that kills Pike) and they worship the wrong kind of people (the kids adore Mapache), real men ride together (Pike, Deke and Mapache each run a posse of sorts), male camaraderie is a good thing (the fiesta binds the bunch together. Also, the attempt to save Angel's life allows the men to experience a nobility they have never felt before), revenge is bittersweet (or, in the Bunch's case, revenge is fatal, since the guys know that killing Mapache will cost them their lives), a man's best friend is his gun (it's hard to imagine Bishop, Engstrum and Co. as anything other than killers), money men are bad! (the railroad exec Harrigan is a greedy, scheming coward), the law is an ass (the band of bounty hunters assigned to Thornton are every bit as low-down as Bishop's boys, the only difference being, they carry a badge), the times they are a-changing (Mapache owns a motor car and the bunch discuss rumours that, somewhere up North, some guys have invented a flying machine), at the end the protagonists ride off into the sunset albeit it in atypical fashion (Sykes and Thornton ride away not to freedom but to face old age together).

Backstory: Perhaps the most remarkable thing about *The Wild Bunch* is that it was never meant to be made. When Warners hired Peckinpah it was to shoot *The Diamond Story*, an action-packed Lee Marvin vehicle. But Marvin was offered a million dollars to star in *Paint Your Wagon* and dropped out, leaving the way for Sam to pitch *The Wild Bunch* script he'd been working on with Walon Green.

The other big story surrounding *The Wild Bunch* concerns the editing. When Peckinpah first cut the movie, it ran 225 minutes. Even he knew that a cut of this length could never be released and so he, Lombardo and Wolfe whittled the film down to 145 minutes. This cut pleased everybody; everybody, that is, except for the test audiences. When *The Wild Bunch* first previewed, people literally ran out of the theatre. Over 70% of the reaction cards were negative, with people describing the film as a revolting work of the sort that should not be visited on a civilised society. Although Sam liked the notoriety that went with having made such a violent film, he didn't want to completely turn off his audience and took it upon himself to take out some of the more 'excessive' sequences. He also willingly edited a few pieces that the Motion Picture Association Of America took exception to.

While he could live with these cuts, Peckinpah couldn't tolerate the changes that were made by Warners' Head Of Production, Ted Ashley. Responding to complaints from theatre owners that the film was too long, Ashley cut out ten minutes of footage, including several crucial flashbacks and the revealing fireside scene. Sam, who was away working on *The Ballad Of Cable Hogue*, was furious with this new cut but was unable to do anything about it since Ashley's version was already playing in cinemas. It would be 1996 before American audiences got to see *the director's cut*.

I use italics here since, in Europe, we've always been able to enjoy what is, more or less, the Peckinpah-approved cut of the film. The 70mm roadshow version of *The Wild Bunch* opened in the UK in August 1969 and has been playing on the art house circuit and network TV ever since. Even this cut doesn't represent Peckinpah's complete vision (the interlude music's missing, together with a few bits of dialogue and the sound of buzzing flies that Sam had wanted to play over the closing credits). However, it's important to understand that what America got excited about back in 1996, we'd been blown away by in 1969.

Peckinpah received his only Academy Award nomination for co-writing the script for *The Wild Bunch*. Sam and fellow writers Roy N Sickner and Walon Green lost out to William Goldman, author of *Butch Cassidy And The Sundance Kid*. Jerry Fielding was also nominated for his magnificent score but was beaten out by Burt Bacharach's contribution to the Newman/Redford buddy Western.

As for what happened on the shoot, read on!

Peckinpah's Posse: The usual suspects, Ballard, Oates, Taylor and Johnson. Sam retained Louis Lombardo's services for *The Ballad Of Cable Hogue* and would hook up with Gordon Dawson for *Bring Me The Head Of Alfredo Garcia*. Composer Jerry Fielding, who had scored Sam's TV movie *Noon Wine*, also became a regular member of Peckinpah's production team (incidentally, *The Wild Bunch* features more music per minute than *The Sound Of Music*).

Posse Members Speak!: Actor L Q Jones: "It was an intense shoot. From day one, it was an intense shoot. Sam lost it on *The Wild Bunch*, but I've seen him worse, like on the set of *Pat Garrett And Billy The Kid*. On *The Wild Bunch*, Sam was so in love with the material and so determined to do a good job, he only lost it when he thought things weren't going according to plan.

"We finished shooting in June 1968. The last day was spent on a sound stage at Churubusco Studios in Mexico City, shooting close-ups. Sam got all of the bunch and a few of us other guys to stand on blocks, so that all they had behind them was the rich blue Mexican sky. Sam shot the footage he wanted and immediately burst into tears! I only ever saw Sam cry twice. *Really* cry. The other times, it was just the drink talking. That day, he wailed like a baby. Why? Because he had given the picture everything and now it was over. If you give as much as Sam gave to *The Wild Bunch*, tears are the only relief, the only thing that makes sense.

"Everyone talks about what a good technical director Sam was, but few people recognise how great a director of actors he was. On *The Wild Bunch*, he coaxed extraordinary work out of people. Eddie O'Brien was thought a blind, drunk has-been by most critics. Then they started talking about how brilliant he was in *The Wild Bunch* and writing that he still had the magic that made him so memorable in *DOA*. And Ernie Borgnine, who'd got a reputation, undeserved in my opinion, of being an old ham since winning his Oscar; in Sam's hands he became a legend all over again. As for us younger guys, Warren, Ben, Strother, Me, we built our careers on having been in *The Wild Bunch*. It opened doors. People who wouldn't return our agents' calls were now asking us out to dinner. Of course, cause we were Sam's boys we'd always go to lunches in our work gear; Stetsons, ponchos, leather jackets. It must have looked weird, us cowboys eating canapés with the suit-and-tie bri-gade."

Screenwriter Walon Green: "It was late 66 and I was working as a documentary film-maker when I got a call from stuntman Roy N Sickner. He'd written a treatment for a Western and he wanted me to turn it into a screenplay. I wrote it and then I passed it on to Sam, who rewrote it.

"When Sam rewrote, he didn't alter a line here and there - he really rewrote. He didn't meddle with the structure so much as with the dialogue. By the time he'd finished, practically all the dialogue had changed. He tinkered with a few scenes too. The sequence where the Bunch cross the river with the stolen guns: in my ver-sion, the river's crossed on a raft, which Sam swapped for a bridge. When I heard that, I said: "Christ, are you going to blow up another bridge?" Sam replied: "It's not just blowing up another bridge. It's about how you blow up the bridge." And he was right. It was terrific. I suppose I should have been pissed off. That sort of rewriting, however, is the kind a screenwriter appreciates."

Editor Louis Lombardo: "Perhaps the funniest thing about the shoot was that the more we shot, the more apparent it became that Bill Holden was impersonating Sam. I told him one day after dallies: "You're doing Sam!" He was running that Bunch just like Sam was running the movie. His gestures, his tone of voice: it was all Sam.

"Sam could be a wild man. He wanted to take his fists to me when he found out that Assistant Director Cliff Coleman had seen the dallies before he had. Coleman was put on a bus back to LA. Sam wasn't too big to admit when he'd been an asshole, though. Once we got through shooting *The Wild Bunch*, he called up Coleman himself and asked if he'd like to work on another movie. I think Cliff ended up doing AD work on 6 or 7 Peckinpah pictures.

"The rough cut of *The Wild Bunch* ran 3 hours and 45 minutes. It played really well at that length. Martin Scorsese saw that cut and said it was the greatest American movie ever made."

Costume Designer Gordon T Dawson: "What I'll always remember about making *The Wild Bunch* is the time right after Sam had finished shooting the big gun battle at Mapache's fortress and he came over and told me to paint all the red blood black. You see, like roses, blood turns black when it dries. So there I was, in the hot midday sun, with my can, getting all sticky with sweat and paint. It was exhausting work, but it was worth it. There really was method to Sam's madness. He wanted everything to look just right."

Assistant Director Cliff Coleman: "Sam was a perfectionist. He was concerned with minute details. He brought a lifetime of experience to the picture and made damn sure things were the way he knew they should be. Put another way: by the time Sam had finished preparing a set, it even smelled right.

"If there was one person who could've given Sam lessons in debauchery it was Emilio Fernandez. Emilio was a true original, a real one-off. I don't know whether this was before or after he'd shot a producer, but there was an awesome aura about the man. He had brought this harem with him, some 50 teenage girls who lived with him at his hacienda outside Mexico City. Yes, Emilio was perfect for the part of the insane scumbag Mapache. And yet without him, we would never have had that brilliant ants-and-scorpions sequence which set the tone for the whole picture. That was Emilio's idea. He used to play that game as a child."

Straight From The Horseman's Mouth: i) Pike: "If they move... kill 'em!" ii) Pike: "I'd like to make one good score and back off." Dutch: "Back off to what?" iii) Pike: "When you side with a man, you stick with him. If you can't do that you're like an animal. You're finished. We're finished." iv) Pike: "What would you do in his (Thornton's) place? He gave his word!" Dutch: "Gave his word to a railroad!" Bishop: "It's his word!" Dutch: "That ain't what counts, it's who you give it to!" v) Don Jose: "We all dream of being a child again, even the worst of us. Perhaps the worst most of all."

Legacy: Remade by Paul Verhoeven as *Flesh & Blood* (1985), *The Wild Bunch* has been referenced in films as diverse as Robert Rodriguez's *From Dusk Till Dawn* (1995), the Alec Baldwin/Meg Ryan rom-com *Prelude To A Kiss* (1993) and John Landis' laugh-lite comedy *!Three Amigos!* (1986). Clips from the film also appear in Oliver Stone's *Natural Born Killers*. Bishop's Bunch is loosely based on the infamous Hole In The Wall Gang, who also provided the inspiration for the aforementioned *Butch Cassidy And The Sundance Kid*. Released the same year as *The Wild Bunch*, the Newman/Redford vehicle cleaned up at the Oscars and the box office, suggesting that the public prefers to see bandits portrayed not as vicious killers but as happy-go-lucky scallywags who ride around on bicycles to Burt Bacharach hits. Compared with Sam's complex work, *Butch Cassidy* looks like a film for children.

The Verdict: *The Wild Bunch* might be many things (one of the finest film of the 60s, a fine allegory for the Vietnam War, a match for anything cooked up by John Ford) but what it isn't is an exercise in gratuitous misogyny and bloodletting. It isn't Peckinpah's finest movie, either, but it's a bona fide masterpiece and if you haven't seen it already, you won't know how to progress in life until you have. 5/5

The Ballad Of Cable Hogue (1970)

Cast: Jason Robards (Cable Hogue), Stella Stevens (Hildy), David Warner (Joshua), Strother Martin (Bowen), L Q Jones (Taggart), Slim Pickens (Ben), Peter Whitney (Cushing), R G Armstrong (Quittner), Gene Evans (Clete), William Mims (Jensen), Susan O'Connell (Claudia), Kathleen Freeman (Mrs Jensen), Vaughn Taylor (Powell), Felix Nelson (William), Max Evans (Webb)

Crew: Director Sam Peckinpah, Writers John Crawford & Edmund Penney, Producer Sam Peckinpah, Executive Producer Phil Feldman, Co-Producer William Faralla, Associate Producer Gordon Dawson (uncredited), Music Jerry Goldsmith, Cinematographer Lucien Ballard, Editors Frank Santillo & Louis Lombardo, Production Manager Dink Templeton, Costume Designer Robert Fletcher, Set Decoration Jack Mills, Assistant Director John Guadioso

Story: Gold prospector Cable Hogue is left to die in the desert by his treacherous partners Bowen and Taggart. Swearing revenge on the duo, Hogue staggers through the spare chaparral for 4 full days before finding an oasis. Delighted just to be alive, Hogue's thoughts quickly turn to the money that's to be made from the watering hole.

Deciding to charge passers-by 10 cents to drink from his spring, Hogue shoots his first customer but befriends the second, itinerant preacher Joshua Sloane. Sloane is a libidinous but likeable old cove who has a thing going with a married woman in the town of Deaddog. Keen to avoid the said lady's husband, Sloane promises to guard the oasis while Cable rides into Deaddog to properly purchase his property. Hogue tries to talk the town's stagecoach manager into investing in the project but the official refuses, leaving Cable to ask the local bank for a loan. Hogue also finds love in the arms of Deaddog's finest whore, Hildy.

Hogue returns to his outpost which, with Sloane's help, he soon turns into a fully functional service station. He is, in turn, joined by Hildy who has been driven out of Deaddog. The pair swiftly fall in love but Hildy is sworn to another and she leaves for San Francisco.

No sooner has Hildy departed than Hogue's former associates Bowen and Taggart appear. Hogue, who has been anticipating their return, snares the pair in a pit and bombards them with rattlesnakes. When Bowen and Taggart eventually scramble out of the pit, Cable shoots the latter in self-defence but spares the pitiable Bowen.

His thirst for revenge slaked, Cable gets back to running his outpost. His sweet life is made sweeter still by the return of the widowed Hildy. So wealthy that she now travels around in a chauffeured automobile, Hildy asks Hogue to retire with her to New Orleans. He accepts but is then accidentally crushed beneath Hildy's car. As Cable lies dying beneath the desert sun, Joshua Sloane pays tribute to his fallen friend.

Themes & Ideas: Fast cutting and slow motion (While *The Wild Bunch* featured slow-motion extravaganzas, *Cable Hogue* contains sequences in which the footage is actually speeded-up. As Benny Hill, Richard Lester and numerous silent comedians realised, speeded-up footage looks funny and *The Ballad Of Cable Hogue* is meant to be a comedy. While Peckinpah's slow-motion sequences feel wholly appropriate, the equally artificial fast-forwarded footage really jars), friendship is a higher value that should never be betrayed but often is (Taggart and Bowen eighty-six their fellow prospector Cable), male camaraderie is a positive thing (Sloane helps Hogue make a go of the watering hole), the times they are a-changing (Sam's least subtle essay on the death of the West, *Cable Hogue*'s tendency towards overwrought symbolism reaches its apotheosis in the scene when the frontiersman dies beneath the wheels of a motorcar), women are trouble (it's Hildy's car that does for Hogue), revenge is bittersweet (Hogue spends the whole movie waiting for Bowen and Taggart, but when they do reappear he only kills Taggart in self-defence and he lets Bowen live), deathbed scenes are super (Cable's passing is an object lesson in how to reach the heart without taking a detour into sentimentality).

Backstory: For such a low-key, laid-back little film, *The Ballad Of Cable Hogue* had an incredibly troubled shoot. The only film Peckinpah both produced and directed, Sam purchased Penney and Crawford's *Cable Hogue* screenplay in 1967 when he was still blacklisted. Peckinpah, who'd substantially rewritten the screenplay, set off for Arizona in the early spring of 1969, confident that he could bring the film in in 7 weeks. When thunderstorms wrecked the first 10 days of shooting, Peckinpah responded by firing crew members in the same unsparing way that his protagonists fire bullets. By the time the film wrapped, Sam had sent 35 people back to Los Angeles.

Peckinpah also got into a tremendous spat with his daughter Sharon over his using real livestock when the script called for animals to be shot. Rabbits, rattlesnakes, gila monsters, birds: Peckinpah had no qualms about killing creatures in the name of entertainment. Sharon, who had been hired to shoot a documentary on the making of the film, got into a blazing row with her father which ended with one of Sam's rare crying fits.

Although *The Ballad Of Cable Hogue* tested positively, Warner Brothers distributed the film with little press coverage and no radio or TV advertising. As co-star Stella Stevens recalled; "Warners didn't release it. They flushed it." Incensed by Warners' refusal to promote *Cable Hogue* and by their hacking apart of *The Wild Bunch*, Peckinpah launched a stinging attack on the studio in the film press. He was rewarded with the immediate termination of his contract.

Peckinpah's Posse: Martin and Jones reprise their double act from *The Wild Bunch* and Armstrong and Pickens saddle up for their third and second Peckinpah pictures, respectively. Jason Robards, meanwhile, had appeared in *Noon Wine*. *Cable Hogue* was also the first of Sam's films to feature David Warner, a well-spoken Englishman who ought to look lost on Peckinpah's prairie but actually blends in perfectly. Sam also retained the behind-the-camera services of Lucien Ballard and Louis Lombardo.

Posse Members Speak: Actor L Q Jones: "I've got fond memories of making *Cable Hogue*. It was a very different film to *The Wild Bunch*, but again, I think we all felt we were making something really important, albeit a lot more sedate.

"It was while Sam was editing *Cable Hogue* that he heard what Warner Brothers had done to *The Wild Bunch*. I'd never seen him so angry. He was glowing with rage."

Editor Louis Lombardo: "*The Ballad Of Cable Hogue* represented a very different challenge to *The Wild Bunch*. It wasn't a question of cutting action scenes in an innovative fashion but of re-enforcing the film's elegiac feel and easy strolling manner. It called for subtlety in the same way that *The Wild Bunch* called for excitement. Thing is, no one ever wants to talk about *Cable Hogue*, but I'm as happy with my work on that movie as I am with what I did on *The Wild Bunch*. They were both rewarding experiences and, in many ways, *The Ballad Of Cable Hogue* was a far greater technical achievement."

Straight From The Horseman's Mouth: Cable Hogue: "Don't make me a saint, but don't put me down too deep."

The Verdict: Although it deals with classic Peckinpah themes, *The Ballad Of Cable Hogue* is stylistically quite different from Sam's other pictures. It's the only Peckinpah film to feature broad comedy, animation (the Indian on a dollar bill winks at Cable when he considers spending it at Deaddog's brothel) and musical numbers (the lengthy 'Butterfly Mornings' montage in which Cable and Hildy sing to one another as they bathe, feed and make love). Unfortunately, this atypical stuff adds nothing and only undercuts the film's finer moments - principally, the glorious story arc that sees Hogue both begin and end the movie dying beneath the vast Arizona sky. Try as it might to embrace the emotions, *Cable Hogue*'s stylistic frailties keep the viewer at arms length. 3/5

Straw Dogs (1971)

Cast: Dustin Hoffman (David Sumner), Susan George (Amy Sumner), Peter Vaughan (Tom Hedden), T P McKenna (Major Scott), Del Henney (Charlie Venner), Jim Norton (Cawsey), Donald Webster (Riddaway), Ken Hutchinson (Norman Scutt), Len Jones (Bobby Hedden), Sally Thomsett (Janice), Robert Keegan (Harry Ware), Peter Arne (John Niles), Cherina Schaer (Louise Hood), Colin Welland (Reverend Hood), David Warner (Henry Niles - uncredited)

Crew: Director Sam Peckinpah, Writers David Zelag Goodman & Sam Peckinpah, Novel The Siege Of Trencher's Farm by Gordon Williams, Producer Daniel Melnick, Associate Producer James

Swann, Music Jerry Fielding, Cinematographer John Coquillon, Editors Paul Davies & Tony Lawson & Roger Spottiswoode & Robert L Wolfe (consultant), Production Designer Ray Simm, Art Director Ken Bridgeman, Production Manager Derek Kavanagh, Assistant Directors Nick Farnes & Terry Marcel

Also Known As: Sam Peckinpah's Straw Dogs

Story: English rose Amy Sumner returns to the village of her birth with her American astrophysicist husband, David. Conscious that the marriage is in trouble, David hopes that the tranquillity of the English countryside will give them both time to reflect on their relationship.

Rather than trying to make the marriage work, David retreats into his books. Amy, starved of attention, takes to flirting with a group of workmen David has hired to repair a barn roof. The labourers respond by ridiculing David's nerdish behaviour. What starts out as gentle teasing ends with the couple finding their pet cat strangled in their bedroom wardrobe. Amy insists that David confront the labourers but he decides instead to befriend them. Remarkably, the young professor hits it off with the locals and accepts their invitation to go on a hunting trip.

The next day, David sets off with the villagers into the wilderness. He is presented with a shotgun which is almost as big as he is and is then told to wait in a meadow while the locals drive the birds towards him. The villagers then desert him.

While David is left waiting for the game birds, Amy is visited by her former lover Charlie Venner. As the two talk about the old times, Venner pounces upon her. Remarkably, even repulsively, Amy gives in, the frustrations of her shallow marriage being so great as to make even an encounter with the brutish Venner tolerable. It's then that a second villager, Norman Scutt, arrives back from the hunt carrying a shotgun. The pair share an awful look and then brutally rape Amy.

David, meanwhile, stands motionless in the forest meadow, still waiting for the birds to take flight...

Because of her conflicting emotions at the time of the attack, Amy decides not to tell David about it. She even accompanies him to a church social event but has to leave early when the memories of the incident start to eat into her mind. On the drive back to the farmhouse David runs over Henry Niles, the village idiot. Niles accidentally killed a girl while attending the same church function. David drives the injured man back to his house and tries to call the doctor. When he gets no reply, he rings the local pub where the dead girl's father, Tom Hedden, is nursing his drink problem. Alerted to Niles' whereabouts, Hedden gathers up the labourers and sets off for the Sumners' residence.

On arrival, the mob demand that David hand Niles over but he refuses, convinced that the locals will kill the retard. The pacifist professor is then left to assemble a crude arsenal of weapons while the villagers lay siege to the house. In the mêlée that follows, David does away with all but Venner who is shot full in the chest by a vengeful Amy. The fight over, Sumner surveys his body spattered home. "Jesus Christ," he gasps "I got them all." Exhilarated, he offers to take Harry Niles home. "I don't know where I live," the idiot murmurs. "That's okay, I don't either," David replies.

Themes & Ideas: Fast cutting and slow motion (not as much as in *The Wild Bunch* but still enough to be effective), ultraviolence (the critic John Naughton wrote that *Straw Dogs,* 'features sundry unpleasantness with a bear trap.' This is a bit like saying *Driller Killer* showcases the inappropriate use of a Black & Decker), real men ride together (the villagers might be a mangy, inbred bunch of shotgun-wielding rapists, but, by heck, do they like being with one another!), revenge is bittersweet (killing the invaders doesn't resolve the conflict within David), a man's best friend is his gun (*Straw Dogs* doesn't so much claim that man was born to battle as suggest that once you've taken up arms, it's almost impossible to return to normalcy. David's final words are the most chilling cinematic representation of the isolating affects of violence this side of the door slamming shut on Ethan Edwards at the end of *The Searchers* (1955, dir John Ford)).

Subtext: Straw Dogs might not take place in Sam's usual settings but the subject matter couldn't be closer to the director's heart. Indeed, the film has a distinct autobiographical edge - David's humiliation on the hunting trip corresponding with the awkwardness Sam confessed to feeling when out shooting with his burly brethren. *Straw Dogs* was also informed by Peckinpah's strongly-held belief that bad things happen to people because they want them to. As he said on *Straw Dogs'* release; "David set it (the rape) up. There are 18 different places in that film where he could have stopped the whole thing. He didn't. He let it go on."

Incidentally, the film's fabulous mood title is taken from a passage in *The Book Of 5,000 Characters* by Chinese philosopher, Lao Tzu.

Backstory: The box-office failure of *The Ballad Of Cable Hogue* left Peckinpah concerned that the career he had worked so hard to re-ignite might soon be snuffed out again. Approaching producer Daniel Melnick with an eye to getting *The Hi-Lo Country* green lit, Sam instead struck a deal to direct a feature based on Gordon Williams' thriller *The Siege Of Trencher's Farm*.

Sam was a very busy boy on the set of *Straw Dogs*. Besides rewriting David Zelag Goodman's screenplay, he got drunk with Ken Hutchinson and got off with both his production assistant and Warner chief Ken Hyman's secretary. His carousing didn't impress Dustin Hoffman who suggested that producer Melnick fire Peckinpah and hire British director Peter Yates. Melnick took one look at Yates' filmography (the stylish but dramatically light *Bullitt*, the Cliff Richard vehicle *Summer Holiday*) and told Sam to keep shooting.

Peckinpah's Posse: It's weird to see a man used to working with Western icons like Warren Oates and L Q Jones directing British TV favourites like Peter Vaughan (*Porridge*), Ken Hutchinson (*Murphy's Mob*) and Sally Thomsett (*Man About The House*). Sam offset the presence of so many unfamiliar faces by hiring David Warner, Robert Wolfe and Jerry Fielding. *Straw Dogs* also features the posse debuts of editor Roger Spottiswoode and John Coquillon, who would become Peckinpah's cameraman of choice following the retirement of Lucien Ballard.

Straight From The Hoffman's Mouth: David: "This is my house! This is where I live! This is mine! Me! I will not allow violence against my house."

Legacy: Straw Dogs' notoriety was exacerbated by the British Board of Film Classification's refusal to grant the picture a video certificate. According to James Ferman, head of the BBFC at the time the decision was made, *Straw Dogs* was one of the films rapists sometimes mentioned when asked to account for their crimes. The validity of this statement is undercut by comments writer/director Paul Schrader made in defence of the violent content of the very excellent *Taxi Driver* (1976, dir Martin Scorsese): "If you censor a film, all you do is censor a film, not confront a problem. These characters are running around and can be triggered off by anything. A few years ago, they did a study about incitement to rape and the thing that cropped up most often was the old Coppertone suntan oil ad. It had a little puppy tugging at a girl's swimsuit. It had just the right mixture for these rapists of adolescent sexuality, female nudity, rear entry, animals, violence." Perhaps now that the BBFC has grown up enough to allow *The Exorcist* a video release, it might not be too long before *Straw Dogs* appears on the shelves of your local Blockbuster.

The scene in which David arms himself has been copied by Mark L Lester (*Commando*), Quentin Tarantino (*Pulp Fiction*) and Chris Columbus (*Home Alone*). So, if you didn't already think this MacCauley Culkin vehicle was pretty tasteless, bear in mind that it homages a film in which a teenage girl is murdered by a mentally-handicapped man, a woman is raped twice in the space of 5 minutes, and a man is almost chopped in half by a bear trap.

The Verdict: I have a friend who believes *Straw Dogs* to be the finest movie of the 1970s. I also have a friend who thinks the film so distasteful, it ought never to have been released. Now that's both of my friends exhausted, I should add that my feelings towards the picture change with the days of the week. On Mondays, Wednesdays and Fridays, I find *Straw Dogs* a chilling, terrifying but utterly compelling study of modern-day masculinity. The rest of the time, I find it so troubling, I prefer not to think about it. If only there wasn't that rape scene, then maybe I could fully embrace *Straw Dogs*. That said, if you took the nasty, fire-and-brimstone, eternal damnation stuff out of *The Bible*, we might not still be talking about it 2000 years after the birth of Christ. Rape or no rape, this is a hard film to like, and an even harder one to rate. 2/5

Junior Bonner (1971)

Cast: Steve McQueen (Junior Bonner), Robert Preston (Ace Bonner), Ida Lupino (Elvira Bonner), Joe Don Baker (Curly Bonner), Barbara Leigh (Charmagne), Mary Murphy (Ruth Bonner), Don 'Red' Barry (Homer Rutledge), Sandra Deel (Nurse Arlis), Rita Garrison (Flashie), Charles D Gray (Burt), Ben Johnson (Buck Roan), Bill McKinney (Red Terwilliger), Matthew Peckinpah (Tim Bonner), Sundown Spencer (Nick Bonner), Dub Taylor (Del)

Crew: Director Sam Peckinpah, Writer Jeb Rosebrook, Producer Joe Wizan, Music Jerry Fielding, Cinematographer Lucien Ballard, Editor Robert L Wolfe

Story: After failing to conquer a monstrous Brahma bull called Sunshine and conceding defeat to his arch-rival Red Terwilliger, professional cowboy Junior Bonner heads for his hometown of Prescott, Arizona, to visit his family and participate in the annual Frontier Day rodeo. He pulls in at the old Bonner ranch house just in time to see it being torn apart by bulldozers.

Junior stops by the antiques shop run by his mother, Elvira Bonner, who brings him up to speed on recent events. The family ranch was sold by Junior's father, Ace, to his younger brother Curly for a knock-down price. Curly is now redeveloping the land for residential purposes. Ace, on the other hand, is laid up in hospital. Junior has important rodeo business to take care of, but he promises his mother that he will visit his father.

Junior arrives at the hospital to find his father asleep. He tells Arlis, Ace's nurse and sometime squeeze, that he will return later and then heads off to the rodeo site to book his rides for the rodeo. Junior also takes time out to have a look at Curly's trailer-park development and to eye up his nemesis, the tonne and a half of bloody-minded bullock that answers to the name of Sunshine.

That evening, the Bonner clan descend on Elvira's for dinner. Curly and his wife Ruth talk endlessly about their new housing development. They've already offered Elvira a trailer and a job running the estate's shop and they now want Junior to come and work for them as a salesman. When Junior turns the job down, Curly tells him that he can't ride bareback forever and he should start thinking about his future. Junior responds by punching Curly so hard, he flies through the dining-room window.

The next day, Junior again visits the hospital but discovers that his father has discharged himself. Junior returns to the rodeo site where he is offered a job working for Buck Roan, but he turns it down. He then catches up with his father at the Frontier Day parade, and learns of Ace's plan to become a gold prospector in Australia. The Bonners spend the rest of the day at the rodeo where Junior rides broncos and participates in the wild milk race with his father.

That evening, the Bonner clan meet up in a local saloon and Curly and Junior spar for a second time. At the end of the evening, Junior takes up with a girl called Charmagne and Ace goes home with the estranged Mrs Bonner! As their women sleep, the Bonner men return to the bar, where Curly and Junior make their peace and Ace drops a bunch at the card table.

Independence Day arrives and with it comes the highlight of the rodeo, the bull riding. Determined to win so that he can stay out on the road, Junior rides Sunshine for the full 8 seconds and scoops the purse. He celebrates with Charmagne before heading over to Prescott's travel agency to buy a one-way ticket to Sydney for his father. Junior drives by Curly's place and calls in on his mother, before driving out of Prescott to the next rodeo and another encounter with a bull called Sunshine...

Themes & Ideas: Fast cutting and slow motion (The opening sequence sees Peckinpah experiment with the multi-image techniques that were in fashion at the time. He actually uses this flashy, rather cumbersome device very well, his experience with slow motion perhaps giving him a better understanding than most of how to combine action with essential plot information), ultraviolence (The destruction of the ranch contains the same energy and savagery as Peckinpah's gunfights), money men are bad (Curly has made his fortune selling off the family silver), friendship is a higher value that should never be betrayed but often is (Curly doesn't just buy the ranch from his father, he refuses to pay the full asking price), women are trouble (we're encouraged to believe that Ruth corrupted Curly, transforming him from a good ol' boy into a bad landowner), the times they are a-changing (Junior's efforts to stand still in a rapidly changing world might be well intentioned but they have left him looking like a dinosaur. In some ways, he is every bit as pitiable as Curly), at the end the protagonist rides off into the sunset albeit in an atypical manner (as Junior drives off towards the horizon, he seems to be heading towards extinction rather than fresh adventure).

Subtext: You don't need a spyglass to see that this is another film about Sam's favourite subject. In some ways, it's the most positive of Peckinpah's 'end of days' tracts as it shows that, although the frontier had been compromised, you could still make a living out of the cowboy life as recently as 1971. The presence of Steve McQueen lends the allegory further power and pathos.

Backstory: Junior Bonner was shot with relatively little incident in Prescott, Arizona. There's an old saying that, "if you've a choice living betwixt Hell and Arizona, live in Hell and rent out Arizona." Prescott, though, is a charming place with a melancholic, town-out-of-time feel, which is presumably why Jeb Rosebrook chose it as the setting for his screenplay.

Peckinpah's Posse: Not too many familiar faces amongst the cast, just Dub Taylor and Ben Johnson. Sam's only son, Matthew Peckinpah, also has a small role as one of the Bonner boys. On the technical side, Ballard, Wolfe and Fielding are on hand to deliver their respective brands of magic. The finest work in the film comes from three Peckinpah irregulars: McQueen (who, despite also appearing in *The Getaway*, is too iconic a figure to be considered a stock player); Joe Don Baker (who has been brilliant in everything from *Charley Varrick* (1973, dir Don Siegel) to the BBC's *Edge Of Darkness*); and Ida Lupino, an extraordinarily talented actress (*High Sierra*, *The Big Knife*) *and* one of Hollywood's first female directors (*The Hitch-Hiker*, *The Bigamist*).

Straight From The Horseman's Mouth: Ruth: "Never was a horse that couldn't be rode. Never was a cowboy that couldn't be throwed."

Legacy: Junior Bonner belongs to that small but respected sub-genre, the Rodeo Western. Similarly themed films include *The Honkers* (1971, dir Steve Ihnat), *J W Coop* (1971, dir Cliff Roberton), *When Legends Die* (1972, dir Stuart Miller) and the Lane Frost biopic *8 Seconds* (1994, dir John G Avildsen). With character names like Terwilliger and Homer, it's also safe to suggest that Matt Groening is a big fan of *Junior Bonner*.

Verdict: There might not be any guns or blood but the mood alone marks this out as a Peckinpah picture. McQueen is on inspired form, mixing his standard slow-burn with a fragility he would not show again until diagnosed with cancer. Lupino's performance, on the other hand, blows clean out of the water the myth that Peckinpah couldn't direct women. Both turns look very small indeed when compared with the way *Junior Bonner* documents the passing of time. Warm but unsentimental, sympathetic but unstinting, the film doesn't just detail the death of Bonner's world, it leaves you with a physical sensation of loss. In short, the sort of film the word 'lyrical' could have been created for. 5/5

The Getaway (1972)

Cast: Steve McQueen (Doc McCoy), Ali MacGraw (Carol McCoy), Ben Johnson (Jack Benyon), Sally Struthers (Fran Clinton), Al Lettieri (Rudy Butler), Slim Pickens (Cowboy), Richard Bright (Thief), Jack Dodson (Harold Clinton), Dub Taylor (Laughlin), Bo Hopkins (Frank Jackson), Roy Jenson (Cully), John Bryson (The Accountant), Bill Hart (Swain), Tom Runyon (Hayhoe), Whitney Jones (The Soldier), Raymond King (Boy On The Train), Ivan Thomas (Boy On The Train), C W White (Boy's Mother), Brenda W King (Boy's Mother), W Dee Kutach (Parole Board Chairman), Brick Lowry (Parole Board Commissioner), Martin Colley (McCoy's Lawyer), O S Savage (Field Captain), Dick Crockett (Bank Guard), A L Camp (Hardware Shop Owner), Bob Veal (TV Shop Proprietor), Bruce Bissonette (Sporting Goods Salesman), Maggie Gonzalez (Carhop), Jim Kannon (Cannon), Doug Dudley (Max), Stacy Newton (Stacy), Tommy Bush (Cowboy's Helper)

Crew: Director Sam Peckinpah, Writer Walter Hill, Novel Jim Thompson, Producers Mitchell Brower & David Foster, Associate Producer Gordon T Dawson, Music Quincy Jones, Cinematographer Lucien Ballard, Editors Robert L Wolfe & Roger Spottiswoode (consultant), Art Directors Angelo P Graham & Ted Haworth, Set Decoration George R Nelson, Costume Designer Ray Summers, Production Manager Donald Guest, Assistant Directors Newt Arnold & Gordon T Dawson & Ron Wright

Story: Having gone wire-happy after 5 years inside, bank robber Doc McCoy begs his wife/accomplice Carol to cut a deal with corrupt politician Jack Benyon and secure his release. Once free, McCoy meets up with Benyon who orders him to rob a local bank with 2 other thieves, Jackson and Butler. McCoy is given just 2 weeks to set up the job.

Doc executes the bust with the military precision that has made him the most wanted bank robber in Texas. Just as it looks as if the crew are going to make off with the money, the unstable Jackson shoots a security guard. During the frantic escape, Jackson is killed by the duplicitous Butler, and Carol and Doc almost come a cropper in a road accident. When the survivors arrive at the rendezvous point, Butler pulls a gun on McCoy but the arch-criminal is a step ahead of him and sends him to his grave. As the McCoys drive away, Butler, who has been wearing a bulletproof vest, gets to his feet and gives chase.

The McCoys arrive at Benyon's ranch and Doc and the politician set about dividing up the loot. When Benyon tells Doc that Carol exchanged sexual favours to gain his release, Mrs McCoy blows the corrupt official away. After they leave the property, Doc savagely beats Carol for her 'betrayal.'

Benyon's body is discovered by his associates. Meanwhile, the injured Butler takes local doctor Harold Clinton hostage, together with his wife Fran, and demands that he be driven to the McCoys' ultimate destination, El Paso.

The McCoys hightail it to the railway station to catch the El Paso train, only for a Stetson-wearing thief to steal the bag containing the money. Doc retrieves the cash but not before battering the burglar and letting some inquisitive children get a good look at his face. Once reunited with Carol, Doc suggests that it might be a good idea if they split up. While the pair spend a frosty night in a motel, the thief and the children on the train shop Doc to the police.

Doc buys a radio to find out how the police investigation is going, but is recognised by the store clerk. Aware that he has been identified, McCoy goes into the shop next door and invests in a shotgun. When the cops summoned by the clerk arrive, Doc blows up their patrol car. He and Carol then dump their own vehicle and catch a Greyhound bus to Dallas.

Once there, the McCoys buy a car and set off for Mexico, only for an ill-advised stop for hamburgers to bring the cops down on top of them again. This time, Carol and Doc escape by hiding out in a dustcart. It's when they're left sitting with the rest of the trash on a garbage dump that Doc realises what Carol is willing to go through to be with him and suggests they start again.

Having now abandoned doctor Clinton and taken up with his wife, Butler arrives at the McCoy's El Paso rendezvous, The Laughlin Hotel. Benyon's posse have also been summoned to the bordello.

When the McCoys check into The Laughlin, they think they're home free. As they sprawl out on the bed with their riches, Butler and Fran arrive posing as room service. Doc knocks out the pair of them and then sets about Benyon's goons. By the time he is through, Doc has killed all the henchman, together with a briefly revived Butler.

Outside the hotel, Doc and Carol hold up an ageing cowboy and demand that he drive them across the border. The couple take such a shine to the good ol' boy that they offer him $30,000 for his truck. While the cowboy walks home to tell his wife the good news, Doc and Carol head south of the border.

Subtext: Peckinpah said that *"The Getaway* is a genre movie. It doesn't have a second act." And it doesn't have a subtext, either.

Themes & Ideas: Fast cutting and slow motion (The opening sequence in which McCoy's crack-up is condensed into a few short minutes is a virtuoso piece of film-making. And while Butler's slow-motion 'death' feels a little overdone, the final gunfight is a prime piece of Peckinpah), ultraviolence (Said finale is an incredibly bloody affair), real men ride together (Benyon runs a posse. Carol and Doc are a lethal combination), the law is an ass (Benyon is as much an outlaw as the McCoys), friendship is a higher value that should never be betrayed but often is (Carol gets into bed with Benyon to secure her husband's release), women are trouble (If sleeping with Benyon wasn't bad enough, Carol misplaces the loot. Fran Clinton is as shrill and annoying as Tiny Tim), a man's best friend is his gun (Doc has bank robbing in his genes), kids are lil' bastards (two boys upset McCoy on the train and then identify him to the police), the times they are a-changing (Doc's task is complicated by new technology such as security cameras), at the end the protagonists ride off into the sunset albeit in atypical fashion (actually, *The Getaway* ends in traditional Western fashion. I only mention this because Jim Thompson's novel has an apocalyptic, hell-in-a-cell finale).

Backstory: Nothing Sam did on the set of *The Getaway* could overshadow Steve McQueen's romancing of Ali MacGraw from beneath the nose of producer Robert Evans. For all his talk about not caring too much for the picture, Peckinpah wasn't able to completely muzzle his perfectionist streak as is illustrated by his sacking of his daughter Sharon for failing to pull her weight.

Peckinpah's Posse: Ben Johnson, Dub Taylor, Slim Pickens (sounding more than ever like Deputy Dawg), Jack Dodson and Bo Hopkins can be found in front of camera, together with new posse member Richard Bright. *The Getaway* also showcased the talents of Lucien Ballard, Robert Wolfe, Roger Spottiswoode and Gordon Dawson. Jerry Fielding also worked on the picture but his score were rejected by McQueen in favour of an incredibly obtrusive offering from Quincy Jones (it sounds like a cross between the themes to *Midnight Cowboy* and *Animal Magic*).

Legacy: Adapted by Walter Hill from the acclaimed novel by Jim Thompson, *The Getaway* was remade in 1994. It wasn't a bad film as remakes go: Kim Bassinger made for a fine Carol McCoy and James Woods and Michael Madsen were brilliant, if a little under-stretched, as the bad guys. But director Roger Donaldson is no substitute for Sam Peckinpah and Alec Baldwin isn't fit to wipe Steve McQueen's ass let alone reprise one of his finest roles. The remake also failed to match the commercial success of the original which grossed $19 million in the US alone.

Verdict: It might be Sam's most impersonal picture but there's still a hell of a lot to like about *The Getaway*. The only disappointment is that Peckinpah couldn't find it in him to grind out a few more studio pictures as it might have allowed him to realise personal projects like *My Pardner* and *The Hi-Lo Country*. Spend some time in the company of Steve McQueen's excellent bad guy made good and these melancholy thoughts soon evaporate. 4/5

Pat Garrett And Billy The Kid (1973)

Cast: James Coburn (Pat Garrett), Kris Kristofferson (Billy The Kid), Bob Dylan (Alias), Jason Robards (Governor Lew Wallace), Richard Jaeckel (Sheriff Kip McKinney), Katy Juardo (Mrs Baker), Slim Pickens (Sheriff Baker), Chill Wills (Lemuel), John Beck (Poe), Rita Coolidge (Maria), R G Armstrong (Deputy Ollinger), Luke Askew (Eno), Richard Bright (Holly), Matt Clark (J W Bell), Jack Dodson (Howland), Jack Elam (Alamosa Bill), Emilio Fernandez (Paco), Paul Fix (Pete Maxwell), L Q Jones (Black Harris), Jorge Russek (Silva), Charlie Martin (Bowdre), Harry Dean Stanton (Luke), Claudia Bryar (Mrs Horrell), John Davis Chandler (Norris), Mike Mikler (Denver), Aurora Clavel (Ida Garrett), Rutanya Alda (Ruthie Lee), Walter Kelley (Rupert), Rudolph Wurlitzer (Tom O'Folliard), Gene Evans (Mr Horrell), Donnie Fritts (Beaver), Elisha Cook Jnr (Cody), Dub Taylor (Josh), Don Levy (Sackett), Sam Peckinpah (Will)

Crew: Director Sam Peckinpah, Writers Rudolph Wurlitzer & Sam Peckinpah (uncredited), Producer Gordon Carroll, Music Bob Dylan, Cinematographer John Coquillon, Editors Roger Spottiswood & Garth Craven & Robert L Wolfe & Richard Halsey & David Berlatsky & Tony de Zarraga, Art Director Ted Haworth, Set Decoration Ray Moyer, Costume Designer Michael Butler, Production Managers Jim Henderling & Alfonsa Sanchez, Assistant Directors Newton Arnold & Lawrence J Powell & Jesus Marin Bello

Story: Flashforward. Black and white. Title Card: 'Near Las Cruces, New Mexico, 1909.' Ageing lawman Pat Garrett is gunned down by his deputy John Poe.

Flashback. Technicolor. Title Card: 'Old Fort Sumner, New Mexico, 1881.' Fresh-faced lawman Pat Garrett rides into Fort Sumner, home of his friend William H Bonney, alias Billy The Kid, the most wanted man in the territory. Garrett tells his buddy that, in 5 days' time, he will become sheriff of the county and it will then be his duty to bring the Kid in. Billy responds to this threat by asking Garrett to: "Stick around. We've still got a few days left."

Once the 5 days are up, Garrett ambushes Billy at his bunkhouse hideout and throws him into Lincoln jail. Garrett then has to leave on business, giving Billy time to escape Lincoln and return to Fort Sumner. When Garrett returns, he hires a posse and goes after the Kid.

Back at Fort Sumner, Billy has a run-in with some bounty killers, who he fends off with some help from Alias, formerly Lincoln's apprentice blacksmith. Taking a lead from his farmer friend Paco, Billy decides to decamp to Mexico.

Garrett, meanwhile, attends a meeting with New Mexico Governor Lew Wallace and some local businessmen. The latter are very keen to see Billy The Kid behind bars and offer Garrett reward money but he throws it back in their faces saying that he will bring in the Kid because it is his duty, rather than his job. After slaying Billy's lieutenant Black Harris, Pat meets the ambitious John Poe and makes him his deputy.

Billy rides south to the border, running into and over Garrett's right-hand man Alamosa Bill Kermitt on the way. On arriving in Mexico, he comes across Paco and his wife taking a beating from one of cattle baron John Chisum's confederates. Billy kills the cowhand then, deciding that Mexico has nothing to offer him, sets off back to Fort Sumner.

Garrett continues his painfully slow pursuit of The Kid. He bumps off most of Billy's associates, before he and Poe team up with Captain Kip McKinney for the final assault on Fort Sumner. Billy, who has made it safely back home, is in bed with his girl when Garrett and Co. arrive. Taking a break from his lovemaking to get some food, The Kid runs straight into Poe, but Pat's deputy is too scared to shoot. Instead, it is left to Garrett to kill his old friend. With Billy dead, Garrett shoots a hole in a mirror and then slumps in a swing chair, spent like one of his bullets. When Garrett rides away from Fort Sumner the next morning, a small boy pelts him with stones.

Flashforward. Black and White. 'Near Las Cruces, New Mexico, 1909.' Ageing lawman is gunned down by his deputy John Poe. The footage of Garrett's murder is interspersed with shots of Billy The Kid.

Subtext: Pat Garrett is by far Peckinpah's most significant Western for, while it laments the passing of old ways, it is actually set during the 'golden days' that the desperadoes in Sam's other movies reminisce about.

The film's myth-busting stance is spelt out in the scene where Garrett becomes involved in a strange bout of target practice with a river boatman. It's one of the smallest moments in the movie and it does absolutely nothing to advance the plot. The contribution to the mood and meaning of the picture, however, is colossal. The dusk setting (the literal 'end of the day'), the melancholic air, the pointless gunfight, the out-of-time warriors: what we have here is the film in miniature. The scene also has a mythic, almost fantasy edge which is appropriate since, in retelling one of the West's greatest tales, *Pat Garrett* seems to suggest that all Westerns, whatever their basis in truth, are fictitious to the point that they might as well begin with the words 'Once Upon A Time....' Indeed, *Pat Garrett* actually begins with a variation on these very words: a title card which reads 'Near Las Cruces, New Mexico, 1909.'

There aren't too many Westerns being made in Hollywood these days, and those that are always assume a revisionist stance (Indians are portrayed as good guys and are never shot, the contribution of women to frontier life is fully acknowledged, etc.). *Pat Garrett*, however, doesn't just appear to be concerned with the Hollywood West of William Wyler or John Ford, it takes issue with historical and academic interpretations of frontier life, too. Not that Peckinpah's film suggests that myth-making is necessarily a bad thing. All *Pat Garrett* seems to be saying is that, through the very act of remembering, we coat the past with a veneer of grandeur, a rich fineness that simply wasn't there at the time. And to appreciate how dazzling that fineness is, just look at Billy The Kid, the romantic hero of so many films and novels, reduced to a shitting, whore-fucking, cheap shot artist in the hands of Sam Peckinpah.

Themes & Ideas: Fast cutting and slow motion (When Garrett takes out The Kid, Billy takes a good 20 seconds to hit the floor), mirrors (Garrett takes a long look at himself when he's at the barber's. Then, straight after he kills The Kid, he blasts a hole in a nearby mirror), ultraviolence (Hard to decide what's more stomach churning: Bob Ollinger literally buying it in a hail of flint and old pennies, or a desperado literally getting it in the neck from Bob Dylan), religious folk are barking mad (One wonders whether R G Armstrong was sponsored to play God-fearing psychos by Save The Children), real men ride together (Billy and Pat both head up posses), children are lil' bastards (a group of kids swing on the gallows that have been built to do away with Billy), and they worship the wrong kind of people (As Garrett rides off after killing The Kid, a small boy pelts him with pebbles), money men are bad (Garrett wants nothing to do with the bounty that's been levied on The Kid or with the people who are willing to pay it), the law is an ass (At one point, Billy explains that there was a time when he carried a badge and Garrett was an outlaw), deathbed scenes are super (It's hard to imagine how Slim Pickens' capitulation could be more moving. Wounded by Black Harris, Pickens hobbles over to the banks of the Rio Bravo, looks one last time at this wife and then stares deep into a world that is dying with him. It's difficult to describe the power of the scene on paper, but then, if you could say everything with words, you wouldn't need cinema in the first place), a man's best friend is his gun (Billy's attempt at going straight is doomed to fail. Garrett, meanwhile, can't shake off his carousing, outlaw ways), the times they are a-changing (the limitless frontier is now all corrals and barbed wire fences. The shop shelves are filled, not with fresh produce, but canned goods. And just in case you haven't got the whole 'times they are a-changing' vibe, Bob Dylan's on hand to spell it out in capital letters), at the end the protagonist rides off into the sunset albeit in atypical fashion (Garrett leaves Fort Sumner a thoroughly despised figure).

Backstory: There is a definite bleary-eyed quality to *Pat Garrett*. This might have something to do with the Kristofferson's habit of drinking a bottle of whisky daily. A second, more convincing explanation concerns Peckinpah's inability to keep his addiction from seeping onto the screen. And one evening, seep onto the screen is precisely what Sam's alcoholism did. Arriving for rushes with a half-drunk bottle of tequila in his hand, a decidedly soused Sam watched the footage he'd shot, staggered up to the screen and urinated all over it.

There have been 3 different cuts of *Pat Garrett* in circulation at one time or another. There's the original theatrical cut which runs 106 minutes, the studio preview which is 124 minutes long and the 'director's cut,' the only version currently available on video, which runs 122 minutes. The weird thing is that the 'director's cut' is actually nothing of the sort. Rescued from the preview suite by Roger Spottiswoode and kept hidden for 20 years, it is, actually, an *early* director's cut, in which a number of the scenes have been loosely edited. This version also lacks a crucial scene between Garrett and his wife that appeared in the studio preview (Despite her absence, Ida Garrett is mentioned in the credits as having been played by Aurora Clavel). The existence of different cuts is problematic since it obliterates the director's true vision, but it's also a source of fun as it means that, whenever you catch the film at the cinema, you're never too sure which cut you're going to see!

Peckinpah's Posse: Hail, hail, the gang's all here: L Q Jones, R G Armstrong, Dub Taylor, Slim Pickens, Jason Robards, Jack Dodson, Richard Bright, Chill Wills, Paul Fix (who first worked with Sam on *The Rifleman*). *Pat Garrett* also features notable posse debuts from Donnie Fritts, Kris Kristofferson, who is excellent if a little old as The Kid, and Walter Kelley, the man who was born to play bar/brothel owner Rupert. Meanwhile, Richard '*Baywatch*' Jaeckel's fine work as the cowardly Kip McKinney leaves you disappointed that he never worked with Sam again. Speaking of Peckinpah, he has a small role as the worldly-wise undertaker Will while screenwriter Wurlitzer pops up as Tom O'Folliard. The crew, meanwhile, features Robert Wolfe, Roger Spottiswoode and Garth Craven, Sam's crack squad of editors, and ace cinematographer John Coquillon.

A Posse Member Speaks: Actor L Q Jones: "*Pat Garrett* was the last film I made with Sam so I suppose it's only natural that I feel sadness about it. The fact I never got to work with him again is nowhere near as upsetting to me as the condition he was in during the making of the movie. When David Weddle interviewed me for his book, I told him that on the first day I arrived on set, I was confronted by this thin, white ghost of a man. It wasn't until he came over and shook my hand that I realised it was Sam. He looked 70 years old and likely to die at any minute.

"He was really drinking by this time. He'd drank a lot in the past, but now you never saw him without a beaker of something in his hand. He was drinking a bottle of grenadine a day, and that was just to whet his appetite. His behaviour had become more random, too. One day, he pulled a gun on Harry Dean Stanton. Another time, he blasted a hole in the mirror in his hotel room. That actually made it into the movie. When Garrett shoots that hole in the mirror at Pete Maxwell's, that was Sam taking pot-shots in his hotel room.

"For about 4 or 5 hours a day though, he was brilliant, as smart and sharp as he had ever been. It was during that time that he made this amazing film. But by the time lunch came, he was shot. And by the time the evening meal was served, it was all he could do to walk home unaided. One night, he complained that the dailies were out of focus. He was actually so drunk that he had double vision."

Straight From The Horseman's Mouth: Garrett: "It feels like... times have changed." Billy: "Times maybe, but not me."

The Verdict: Okay, so it's a bit ragged and a little contrived (Billy discovering the dying Paco is the kind of outlandish coincidence you usually only find in dime novels). But *Pat Garrett And Billy The Kid* has the balls and the breadth of vision to comment upon the West as it was and as it has been captured on film and, for this reason alone, it is Peckinpah's finest picture and one of the genre's greatest films. 5/5

Bring Me The Head Of Alfredo Garcia (1974)

Cast: Warren Oates (Bennie), Gig Young (Quill), Isela Vega (Elita), Robert Webber (Sappensly), Helmut Dantine (Max), Emilio Fernandez (El Jefe), Kris Kristofferson (Paco), Chano Ureta (Bartender), Jorge Russek (Cueto), Don Levy (Frank), Tamara Garina (Grandmother Moreno), Farnesio de Bernal (Bernardo), Ahui Camancho (El Chavito), Monica Miguel (Dolores de Escomiglia), Juan Miguel Diaz (Paulo), René Dupeyron (Angel), Yolanda Ponce (Yolo), Juan Jose Palacios (Juan), Manolo (Tourist Guide), Neri Ruiz (Maria), Roberto Dumont (Chavo), Donnie Fritts (Biker - uncredited)

Crew: Director Sam Peckinpah, Writers Gordon T Dawson & Sam Peckinpah, Story Frank Kowalski, Producer Martin Baum, Executive Producer Helmut Dantine, Music Jerry Fielding, Cinematographer Alex Phillips Jnr, Editors Garth Craven & Sergio Ortega & Robbe Roberts, Art Director Agustin Ituarte, Production Managers William Davidson & Carlos Terron Garcia, Assistant Directors William Davidson & Jesus Marin Bello

Also Known As: Traigamme La Cabeza De Alfredo Garcia

Story: Landowner El Jefe tortures his daughter to find out who impregnated her. Appalled to discover that the father is cowhand Alfredo Garcia, El Jefe offers a million dollars to the man who brings him Garcia's head. El Jefe's henchmen search the width and breadth of Mexico, eventually winding up in a bar in some wretched tourist trap. There, they strike up a conversation with the piano player Bennie, and ask if he knows of Garcia. Bennie pleads ignorance but promises to ask around.

Knowing full well who Garcia is, Bennie visits his girlfriend Elita, a prostitute who also had a thing going with Alfredo, and demands to know where he is hiding. Elita breaks down and tells Bennie that Garcia died in a road accident and has been buried in a town some miles away. After finding out how much Al's head is really worth, Bennie buys a big knife and sets off to dig up the body. Since it's a nice day, he takes Elita with him to do the job. They are followed on their travels by a couple of shady gentlemen.

After a run-in with a vicious pair of bikers, Bennie and Elita arrive at the graveyard. A spiritual woman, Elita is appalled by what Bennie is about to undertake, but her love for her boyfriend leads her to take part in the grave robbing. It is a mistake she will not live to regret for even as Bennie cuts off Garcia's head, both he and Elita and bludgeoned by the aforementioned shady gentlemen.

Bennie comes round to find Elita dead and the head missing. Distraught, he vows revenge on the killers and roars off in his battered auto. Meanwhile, the Garcia family discover what has happened to the grave of their favourite son and set off in pursuit of Bennie and the severed head.

Bennie catches up with his assailants, who have suffered a flat tyre, and dispatches them with ruthless efficiency. Recovering the head, he looks all set to retrieve his reward when he runs into the entire Garcia clan. Things look black for Bennie until El Jefe's favourite homosexual hit men, Quill and Sappensly, roll up. Posing as lost tourists, the duo massacre the Garcias. They try and murder Bennie too but he is too quick for them. Bennie leaves the mountain of bodies behind him and heads for home.

After a restless night, Bennie heads to the hotel where El Jefe's other heavies are holed up and sends them to sleep with Quill and Sappensly. He then journeys to El Jefe's hacienda. The landowner is in excellent spirits; not only has his grandchild just been christened but he now has the head of Al Garcia. He ushers Bennie into his study where he presents him with a suitcase full of cash. Aware of exactly how much Garcia's head has cost, Bennie ignores the money and blows away El Jefe's henchmen. He now has the landowner at his mercy but it is only when El Jefe's daughter insists her brutal father dies that Bennie pulls the trigger.

With the case of money in one hand and the basket holding Al's head in the other, Bennie gets into his car and speeds away. No sooner has he burst through the fortress gates than he is ambushed by El Jefe's gauchos. Helpless, Bennie dies in a hail of bullets.

Subtext: If you ever wanted to know what Sam Peckinpah was like, watch *Bring Me The Head Of Alfredo Garcia*. It won't tell you the whole story. You won't learn about his tough childhood, or his time in the Marines or his film-making heyday. But if you want to know the condition Sam was in in 1974, check out the remarkable performance Warren Oates gives as the washed-up, beat-down Bennie.

The 4 years following the completion of *The Wild Bunch* had been pretty tough on Peckinpah. A big drinker throughout his adult life, he had now succumbed to full-blown alcoholism. His career had also fallen into ill-health. Alex Cox remarked on *Moviedrome* that: "Bennie is quite likely how Peckinpah saw himself, a hired gun, burned out, beaten down, consorting with prostitutes." As Cox added: "The fact that he was able to make a film as mad and personal as *Bring Me The Head Of Alfredo Garcia* means that this wasn't so, but no matter. Bennie was how Peckinpah saw himself in 1974 and it was how he was to become shortly afterwards, a little pimp and odd job man for much richer degenerates."

Alfredo Garcia's 'one-man-against-the-world' scenario also seems to reflect Sam's attitude towards the film-making process.

Themes & Ideas: Real men ride together (El Jefe runs an army of bandidos. The Garcia family travel in a pack. Bennie perishes because he works alone), fast cutting and slow motion (Sam's use of slow motion in *Alfredo Garcia* feels a little laboured. His action sequences, however, are as sharp and exciting as ever), mirrors (On 4 occasions, Bennie lingers over the reflection of his ravaged face), revenge is bittersweet (All the killing in the world won't bring Elita back), a man's best friend is his gun (Bennie can't play the piano for shit but he sure knows how to shoot), the times they are a-changing (while most of the picture takes place in locations that wouldn't look out of place in a Western, the hotel where El Jefe's goons lay up resembles something out of *The Brady Bunch*), children are lil' bastards (a Mexican kid makes a nuisance of himself trying to find out what Bennie has in his bag. "Dead cat," Bennie replies).

Backstory: A man for whom the severing of his umbilical cord was but the first of a thousand unanticipated cuts, Sam must have been elated when he was allowed to oversee the editing of *Alfredo Garcia*. He was given a lot of say-so over the casting and locations, too. It was this artistic freedom that lead Peckinpah to say of *Alfredo Garcia*: "I did the film and I did it exactly the way I wanted to. Good or bad, like it or not, that was my film."

Alfredo Garcia is also the only one of Sam's post *Wild Bunch* films that he didn't direct under the influence of alcohol. As Peckinpah recalled: "My doctor told me I had to quit drinking when I started *Bring Me The Head Of Alfredo Garcia*, so I quit. I started smoking marijuana."

Peckinpah's Posse: Given that *Alfredo Garcia* is such a personal picture, it's surprising just how few of Peckinpah's confederates worked on the production. Of the cast, only Oates, Kristofferson, Donnie Fritts and Fernandez worked for Sam with any frequency while the only familiar faces amongst the technical staff are co-writer Dawson, editor Garth Craven and composer Jerry Fielding.

At least Fernandez was around to entertain Peckinpah during the evenings. There's no mention of whether he brought his harem of nymphets with him, but it's hard to imagine Emilio Fernandez being anything other than exciting to be around. This is, after all, a man who shot a producer in a fit of pique. How Sam must have fantasised about following suit when making *Major Dundee*. And *The Wild Bunch*. And *Pat Garrett And Billy The Kid*. Sadly, Sam and Emilio never got a chance to hook up again as the Mexican director was sent to prison in 1975 for shooting a farm worker who accidentally wandered into shot while Fernandez was filming.

A Posse Member Speaks: Co-writer Gordon Dawson: "Frank Kowalski had been talking to Sam for some time about this idea for a film about a Mafia Don who puts a million dollar bounty on the head of the man who deflowered his daughter, only for you to then discover that the guy's already dead, so whoever's going to get the money is going to have to dig him up. It was a slight idea, but Sam liked it, we worked on the script together, he changed the Mafioso into a Mexican grandee, he liked it a whole lot more and he made it. It wasn't the most complex film that Sam made, at least it didn't seem to be. Now, everyone looks at it as the closest we're ever going to come to a Peckinpah autobiography. I'm glad people are paying the film so much attention, now. I honestly believe that it's one of the best films of the 1970s and it's right up there with the best of Sam's pictures."

Straight From The Hell-Bent Man's Mouth: i) Bennie: "Don't worry, if he's alive I'll find him (Garcia). Sappensly: "Alive isn't our problem." Bennie: "How about dead or alive? How about that?" Quill: "Dead. Just dead." ii) Bennie: "Nobody loses all the time." iii) Bennie (upon shooting a man who is already dead) says to himself: "Why? Because it feels so God damn good." iv) Bennie: "Alfredo's the saint. The saint of our money. I'm gonna borrow a piece of him."

Legacy: For a film that few people have seen, it's surprising how often *Alfredo Garcia* is referenced in pop culture. Besides lending its moniker to laugh-free Rik Mayall comedy *Bring Me The Head Of Mavis Davis* (1997, dir John Henderson), it's hard to imagine an edition of Radio 4's *I'm Sorry, I Haven't A Clue* in which Peckinpah's movie isn't used to comic effect. The mention of the movie also raises a smile in the very funny Chevy Chase comedy (not an oxymoron) *Fletch* (1985, dir Michael Ritchie). In 1992, LA punk band Los Alamos recorded a song entitled 'Bring Me The Rest Of Alfredo Garcia.' Now there's an idea for a sequel...

At the beginning of the film, Quill says that his name is Fred C Dobbs. Fred C Dobbs also happens to be the name of the desperado played by Humphrey Bogart in John Huston's *Treasure Of The Sierra Madre*, a film that shares many thematic concerns with Peckinpah's picture.

Bring Me The Head Of Alfredo Garcia made film critic Harry Medved's list of the 50 worst movies ever made. Harry's brother, Michael, you might remember, is the man who blamed *The Little Mermaid* for the decline of 20th century civilisation.

Verdict: *Bring Me The Head Of Alfredo Garcia* is a film of contrasts. It's the most masochistic piece of film-making this side of Bob Fosse's *All That Jazz*, but it grants Sam's alter ego, Bennie, nobility in death. It looks and feels like a B-movie but it contains the performances and emotional power of an A-picture. The tagline screamed "It's got guts," but it also has heart to spare. And while it suggests the extent of Sam's day-to-day dysfunction, *Alfredo Garcia* proves that he was a director without equal. 5/5

The Brown Dirt Cowboy

Since *Bring Me The Head Of Alfredo* Garcia was the last film Peckinpah made with Warren Oates, now is as good a time as any to shine the spotlight on Sam's favourite actor and on-screen alter ego.

The finest character actor of his or anybody else's generation, Warren Oates looked like a cross between Emilio Zapata and the post-pilsz George Best. "I already had my bath!" he bellowed when questioned about his hygiene in Peckinpah's *Major Dundee*, but to look at Oates in any of his 40-odd movies, it's hard to believe he'd even heard of the concept of water. A surly, unsanitary mess of a man, Oates came to own outright the franchise on thugs, derelicts and degenerates. While his early career consisted of playing Western inbreds and bandits, he later successfully turned his hand to comedy, action pictures and social dramas. With a handsome face lurking behind the Zapata moustache and shaggy mane, he was literally a whisker away from being a leading man. Luckily for us, Warren Oates kept the stubble and became that which we seldom see any more, a truly great character actor.

Director Alex Cox once wrote that; "if you talk to a really good American actor working today, like Dennis Hopper, Harry Dean Stanton or Ed Harris, and ask who they think is the best American actor, living or dead, it is quite likely they're not going to say Marlon Brando. They'll tell you it's Warren Oates!" This being the case, why don't you ever hear Oates' name mentioned in the same breath as the Hollywood greats? The reason has a lot to do with the times we live in. The 1990s have been dominated by superstars and multi-million dollar movies. It's only very recently that, thanks to the wonderful, weirdo, independent pictures coming out of America, audiences have grown used to seeing genuine character actors again. But while his name might not be up there with Brando's, Dean's and Montgomery Clift's, Warren Oates was every bit as good as all of them.

Born in 1928 in Depoy, Kentucky, Warren Oates worked as a manual labourer before he moved into screen acting. He got his earliest breaks on television, appearing in episodes of *The Outer*

Limits, *The Fugitive*, *Lost In Space* and *The Rifleman*. The director of the latter series, one David Samuel Peckinpah, was so impressed with Oates that he promised to use him again, and sure enough, once Warren had made the move to the big screen with small roles in second-rate movies (*Up Periscope*), Sam hired him to play the diseased Henry Hammond in *Ride The High Country*.

In truth, any actor could have played the part of the inbred gold prospector, but few could or would have brought such sincerity to the role. In Warren's hands, Hammond isn't a caricature but a real person, as capable of fraternity as of horrifying violence. For turning an underwritten character into a fully rounded human being, Peckinpah rewarded Oates with a wonderful big-screen entrance - a tight close-up of Warren with a smile on his lips and a crow on his shoulder.

A string of performances in Burt Kennedy Westerns had cemented Oates' reputation as a thug-for-hire by the time he saddled up with Peckinpah again to shoot *Major Dundee*. As Confederate deserter O W Hadley, Oates found himself cast alongside fellow Hammonds L Q Jones and John Davis Chandler. Once again, the role didn't make huge demands on his talents - he simply had to stand around and look surly. When it came to doing nothing on camera, few did it as well as Warren Oates. He might not have had the grandstanding screen presence of a De Niro or Pacino but, with his map-of-Mexico face and gap-toothed grin, Oates was equally capable of lighting up a screen.

For Oates, however, *Major Dundee* wasn't an exercise in screen presence but a chance to fashion another 3-dimensional character from minimal material. During his only scene of any length, Oates displays as many aspects of Hadley's character as possible. Cowardice, loyalty, vivacity, boorishness. Oates puts it all on display in a bravura piece of acting, made all the more remarkable by the fact that i) the scene is very short and ii) he has to share his screen time with the film's stars, Charlton Heston and Richard Harris.

After *Dundee* wrapped, Warren, ever keen to stretch himself, signed on for the role of gunslinger Willet Gashade in Monte Hellman's existential Western *The Shooting*. A minor hit in the US, *The Shooting* and its sister film *Ride In The Whirlwind* were hugely successful in France. Indeed, Parisian film critics were amongst the first people to cotton on to the talent of Warren Oates. What the French knew instinctively, the greater American public would only become aware of subsequent to the release of Sam Peckinpah's genre reshaping Western, *The Wild Bunch*.

After serving Warren a couple of lean roles in their earlier films together, Peckinpah gave Oates a whole bunch of stuff to sink his teeth into when he cast him in the role of the younger, dumber Gorch brother, Lyle. Indeed, with retrospect, it's possible to see the undernourished workouts Warren had to go through on *High Country* and *Major Dundee* as examinations to see whether he had what it took to play what is arguably *The Wild Bunch*'s most complex role.

It has been suggested that amidst all the bloodshed and bullets, there is a love story fighting its way out of *The Wild Bunch*, a tender tale of Bunch-leader Pike's affection for his friend Dutch. However, this subtle study of friendship is, in this writer's opinion, secondary to the camaraderie displayed by the brothers Gorch. Tough without being heartless, sensitive without being homoerotic, the relationship between Tector (Ben Johnson) and the younger, dumber Lyle (Warren Oates) is characterised by the new-anderthal qualities that these fine actors brought to all their roles.

Fraternal affection isn't the only thing that makes Lyle special, however. While the rest of the bunch grow old over the course of the film, he actually grows up, transforming before our very eyes from a reckless, feckless psychopath to the responsible man whom Bishop asks for endorsement when he decides to rescue Angel ("Let's go," snarls Bishop. "Why not?" Lyle concurs). And while William Holden might be doing a damn fine impersonation of Peckinpah's mannerisms, it's Lyle's behaviour (drinking, whoring, fighting) that most closely resembles the director's. This isn't to say that Lyle Gorch is based upon Sam. When, 5 years later, Peckinpah *did* make a film about himself, it was no great surprise that Oates was the man he chose to play the lead.

It was in the wake of his top turn in *The Wild Bunch* that Warren Oates came closest to achieving genuine stardom. In 1974, he landed his first out-and-out lead in John Milius' remake of

Dillinger. A supporting actor for almost a decade, Oates was anxious to make the most of the opportunity he had been afforded. He didn't disappoint. Oates' Dillinger was more sensitive, complex and compelling that any of the gangster's previous screen incarnations. With old friend Ben Johnson outstanding as star-struck G-Man Melvyn Purvis and great support from Richard Dreyfuss and Harry Dean Stanton, *Dillinger* ought to have been a huge box-office hit. Indeed, if it had been handled correctly, it might even have outgunned the thematically similar *Pat Garrett And Billy The Kid*. However, Milius overplayed his hand, the film sank without trace and Oates' career as an orthodox Hollywood leading man was over before anyone could say 'Andrew McCarthy.'

Not that this failure seems to have bothered Oates. Looking back at his career, you get the distinct impression that film, or more precisely fame, was never particularly important to Warren. Weirdo peripheral pictures seemed to have much greater appeal to him than the big-budget action films he could so easily have found parts in. Indeed, after a nice, scene-stealing cameo as Sissy Spacek's sign-painter father in Terrence Malick's *Badlands*, Oates reunited with his compadre Peckinpah to make *Bring Me The Head Of Alfredo Garcia*. Warped, brilliant, bizarre, horrifying; practically all the terms that have been used to describe Peckinpah's heavily autobiographical picture could be used to sum up the breathtaking, to-the-edge performance given by Oates. Such was his gift for playing everyman figures, Oates was even able to make a pathetic loser like the bounty-obsessed Bennie seem pretty noble. In Oates' hands, Bennie isn't just a washed-up barfly. He is a man of contradiction; violent, sure, but also tender and compassionate. You can certainly understand why Sam hired Oates to play his alter ego. Peckinpah's masochism might have driven him to make a film about his personal dysfunction, but his vanity led him to cast an actor whose talent would guarantee that he retained a shred of nobility. Warren's performance is even more incredible when you consider that Bennie spends almost the entire film wearing shades, thus depriving the actor of any opportunity to use his eyes as a means of expression.

Soon after *Alfredo Garcia* wrapped, Oates signed up for Monte Hellman's *Cockfighter* (aka *Born To Kill*) and another demanding role. As Bennie, Warren had his eyes hidden. As Frank Mansfield, a disgraced cockfighter who takes a vow of silence, he lost his voice. In successive films, Oates found himself stripped of the tools that are the very essence of acting. Handicapped as he was, this second, more debilitating restriction did not prevent the actor from turning in his finest screen work. Sadly, *Cockfighter* is seldom shown in the US and is banned in the UK, meaning that the work of both director and leading man has never received the credit it deserves. To get some idea of how remarkable Oates' performance is, read the Charles Willeford novel on which the film is based. That Hellman was able to turn the book into a film is incredible. That Oates managed to turn Mansfield into a layered, 3-dimensional character is as great an acting feat as any this writer cares to remember.

After the bonanza of 1974, Oates returned to the Westerns and B-movies in which he had first made his name. He was one of the few people who could name two of the films Peter Fonda made after *Easy Rider* on the grounds that he was actually in a couple: the weird acid Western *The Hired Hand*; and the holidaymakers versus Satan worshippers actioner *Race With The Devil*. Solid performances as a well-dressed bank robber in William Friedkin's *The Brinks Job* and a weary gunslinger in Hellman's post-pasta Western *China 9, Liberty 37* further proved that, even when the pictures he appeared in weren't up to much, Warren Oates was always very watchable.

By the late 1970s, ill-health and a shortage of good roles had forced Oates to ration out his film appearances. Towards the end of his life, his screen work was restricted to cameos in the comedies *Stripes* and *1941*, and action pictures *Blue Thunder* and *Tough Enough*, and leads in TV remakes of *True Grit* and *The African Queen* (no prizes for guessing which part he played in that one). Then, in 1982, just when Hollywood seemed to have no further need for character actors, Warren Oates died of a heart attack. He was 54.

It's easy to look impressive opposite really great actors. For Warren Oates, there were few opportunities to bask in the talent of his co-stars. As the critic Joanne Walker said of his superb performance as 'G.T.O.' in *Two-Lane Blacktop*; "how do you manage to look good when your co-stars are the lead singer of the James Taylor quartet and one of The Beach Boys?" How indeed? Whatever Warren's secret was, he took it to his grave.

Monte Hellman's highly original take on Warren Oates was that he looked like "a battered, saggy-eyed, hard-drinking Henry Fonda." Compare Oates as Bennie to the moustachioed Fonda that appeared in *My Darling Clementine* and you can see what the director was getting at. The actors' physical similarities are, however, at odds with the symbolic importance of these two artists. In his prime, Henry Fonda was the identikit of the ideal American: wealthy, clean, well-to-do, law-abiding, God-fearing. Come the 1970s, Watergate, Vietnam and the assassinations of Martin Luther King Jnr and the Kennedys had left America and John Q Citizen very different creatures. The effects of corruption and double-cross were writ large in the leer, filthy mane and craven eyes of Warren Oates. In *Dillinger*, John Milius played upon these contrasting images by having Oates re-enact the barn dance sequence from *My Darling Clementine*. Of course, when Fonda square-danced it was as lawman Wyatt Earp. Oates, on the other hand, hoofs it up while playing public enemy number one, John Dillinger.

In an interview, Warren Oates defended Sam Peckinpah stating that; "I don't think he's a horrible maniac. It's just that he injures your innocence and you get pissed off about it." As the critic David Thomson has noted, the actor could have been talking about himself. As great a talent as he was, Warren Oates' appeal and importance cannot be measured simply in terms of acting. As a thug or a bully, cowhand or hired gun, bank robber or cockfighter, Warren Oates gave the American movie-going public a chance to look at itself, to see what it had become in the years between Korea and Grenada. Tragically, introspection has never been one of America's nor Hollywood's finest qualities and so Oates' importance wasn't fully appreciated until years after his death. While he might no longer be with us, Warren Oates' spirit lives on, both in his impressive body of work and in the performances of Steve Buscemi, Tracey Walter, Lance Henriksen, Tim Roth and the 101 other actors who have breached the copyright on his blend of charm, scruffiness and psychosis.

Warren Oates is dead. Viva the Brown-Dirt Cowboy!

The End Of Days

The critical and box-office failures of *Pat Garrett And Billy The Kid* and *Bring Me The Head Of Alfredo Garcia* seemed to kill something inside Sam Peckinpah, and in the years that followed, he only displayed brief flashes of the brilliance and breadth of vision that had made him one of America's finest post-war film-makers.

The Killer Elite (1975)

Cast: James Caan (Mike Lockren), Robert Duvall (George Hansen), Arthur Hill (Cap Collins), Bo Hopkins (Jerome Miller), Mako (Yuen Chung), Burt Young (Mac), Gig Young (Laurence Weyburn), Tom Clancy (O'Leary), Tianna Alexandra (Tommie), Walter Kelley (Walter), Kate Heflin (Amy), Sondra Blake (Josephine), Carole Mallory (Rita), James Wing Woo (Tao Yi), George Cheung (Bruce), Hank Hamilton (Hank), Victor Sen Yung (Wei Chi), Tak Kubota (Negato Toki), Rick Alemany (Ben Otake), Johnnie Burrell (Donnie), Billy J Scott (Eddie), Simon Tam (Jimmy Fung), Arnold Fortgang (Doctor), Tommy Bush (Sam The Mechanic), Matthew Peckinpah (Mat), Eddy Donno (Fake Officer), Kim Kahana (Association Guard), Eddie White (Security Policeman), Gary Combs (Security Policeman), Wilfred Tsang (Wiflie), Wilton Shoong (Wiltie), Alan Keller (Cop), Charles Titone (Solider At Party), Joseph Glenn (Man At ComTeg), Eloise Shoong (Eloise), Mel Cenizal (Waiter), Kuo Lien Ying (Tai Chi Master), Helmut Dantine (Vorodny)

Crew: Director Sam Peckinpah, Writers Marc Norman & Stirling Silliphant, Novel *Monkey In The Middle* by Robert Rostand, Producers Martin Baum & Arthur Lewis, Executive Producer Helmut Dantine, Music Jerry Fielding, Cinematographer Philip H Lathrop, Editors Monte Hellman & Tony de Zarraga & Garth Craven (supervisor), Production Designer Ted Haworth, Set Decoration Rick Gentz, Costume Designer Ray Summers, Production

Manager William Davidson, Assistant Directors Newt Arnold & Jim Bloom & Cliff Coleman & Ron Wright

Story: Mike Lockren and George Hansen work for ComTeg, a San Francisco-based organisation that takes on the jobs the CIA turns down. Mike is a real ladies' man and can do lots of press-ups. George isn't and can't.

Mike and George are close friends. At least, they are until the day George kills one of their charges and maims his partner. Gunshot wounds to the knee and elbow leave Mike with months of rehab ahead of him. ComTeg's chiefs Weyburn and Collins offer Mike a retirement plan, but he turns in down, promising instead to return to the organisation and bring in his former friend. To aid his recovery, he takes up martial arts and jogging. He also takes up with his therapist, Amy.

Meanwhile, CIA bod O'Leary asks ComTeg to guard Japanese politician Yuen Chung during a short stay in America. Since the oriental was almost assassinated on his arrival in the States, Collins is unwilling to take the job but Weyburn, on hearing that George Hansen was part of the assassination party, contracts it out to Mike on a freelance basis.

Mike has, by now, made the sort of recovery Douglas Bader would be proud of. A nunchuck-wielding killing machine, he aligns himself with agents Miller and Mac, which is a strange decision since Miller is mad, Mac is retired and the pair can't stand one another. Still, Mike has the men he wants and he calls Collins to confirm the job. At the time he takes the call, Collins is in a stripclub talking business with Yuen Chung's arch-enemy, ninja master Negato Toki, and George Hansen!

Mike, Mac and Miller visit Yuen Chung at his apartment and arrange to take him to a safe house. As they leave, the group are ambushed by George, but manage to make their escape when the police arrive. With Yuen Chung holed up in a building by the harbour, Mike calls Collins who agrees to let Mike use his yacht to reach the rendezvous point. Collins then gives this information to George.

That evening, George captures Yuen Chung's daughter by the waterside. When Mike tries to intervene, George asks him to join

Collins' side since the pay's so much better. Instead of answering, Mike walks away, leaving George to take one in the back from Miller. Mike calls ComTeg about Collins' betrayal and is told by Weyburn that he can have Collins' job if he sees to him the following day.

The next morning, Mike, Mac, Miller and the Orientals sail to the rendezvous, where they find Collins, Negato and an army of ninjas laying in wait. In the battle that follows, Yuen Chung downs Negato, Miller is fatally wounded, Mike maims Collins and Mac does for the martial artists. With the war over, Weyburn arrives to offer Mike Collins' old position but, now aware that he has been used to resolve a management power struggle, Mike turns the job down and sails away with his old ally Mac in search of new adventures.

Subtext: Like *The Getaway*, *The Killer Elite* is a one-dimensional genre movie. Actionful it might be, but layered it ain't.

Themes & Ideas: Fast cutting and slow motion (In a brilliant sequence, Peckinpah interrupts O'Leary's account of the airport fight with footage of the incident. Oh, and if you've ever wanted to see a ninja fall off a ship in slow motion, this is the film for you), friendship is a higher value that should never be betrayed but often is (Mike is done in by his partner), a man's best friend is his gun (Virtually everybody in the film is a professional killer), women are trouble (A girl gives Lockren the clap. Yuen Chung's daughter almost gets herself and everybody else killed), children are lil' bastards (Yuen Chung's daughter is a pain in the ass), the law is an ass (In the world of modern espionage, there are no good and bad guys, just good and bad payers).

Backstory: It was while shooting *The Killer Elite* that Sam Peckinpah discovered cocaine. According to David Weddle, James Caan was heavily into the Bolivian marching powder and was happy to share his supply with the cast and crew. Sam, never one to shy away from a new narcotic, didn't need asking twice. By the end of the shoot, he was completely hooked.

As on virtually all of his movies, Peckinpah went to war with the producers, paying them back for their refusal to let him rewrite the script by letting his PA direct certain scenes.

Peckinpah's Posse: None of Sam's favourite foot soldiers appear in *The Killer Elite*, but affiliates Bo Hopkins and Gig and Burt Young show their faces as does the wonderful Walter Kelley. Producer Helmut Dantine, who played Max in *Bring Me The Head Of Alfredo Garcia*, also appears as the doomed Vorodny. Behind the scenes, Jerry Fielding provides the score and Garth Craven oversees the editing. As for Monte Hellman, Peckinpah repaid his debt to the editor by appearing as charismatic dime novelist Wilbur Olsen in the post-pasta Western *China 9, Liberty 37* (aka *Clayton Drumm*, aka *Gunfire*, aka *Love, Bullets & Frenzy*).

A Posse Member Speaks (aka Straight From The Hellman's Mouth): Editor Monte Hellman: "Sam had real presence. You knew he was on set even if you couldn't see him. I know a lot of people thought he was past it by the time he came to make *The Killer Elite*, but we all felt he was still a real force. Of course, I'd seen everything he'd made and even though we'd been in movies about the same length of time, I was still trying to learn things from him.

"If working with Sam wasn't a big enough thrill, there was a lot for us to get our teeth into as far as the editing was concerned. Cutting the big airport fight scene around the CIA man's report was very challenging and I think we carried it off well. Naturally, Sam couldn't do everything he wanted, but he liked the flourishes we added. And we found subtle ways to undercut the picture which upset the producers and delighted Sam.

"We got on well. No one got on with Peckinpah all the time, but most days we were on friendly terms. He had a real Western aura about him. I guess he acquired it from all the run-ins he'd had with the producers he'd pissed off or been pissed on by. He felt like an outlaw which was appropriate seeing as how that's who he liked to make movies about. And that's why I cast him in *China 9, Liberty 37*. I got him to play the novelist which worked well as Sam was a great storyteller and had fabulous charisma. He was a good actor, too, but then you could guess that from all the fine performances he'd got out of people over the years."

Straight From The Hard Man's Mouth: i) Mike: "CIA - Circumcised Italian Americans." ii) Mike (To Miller): "You're not a psycho. You're the patron poet of the manic depressives." iii) George:

"Always operate on six key principles: proper planning prevents piss poor performance." iv) Mike: "Don't know where we're going. Don't know where we've been. But where we were wasn't it."

Legacy: With its slow-motion montages and oriental villains, *The Killer Elite* seems to explain why comparisons are occasionally made between Peckinpah and Hong Kong director John Woo (see 'Peckinpahesque Movies').

Verdict: It's a measure of Peckinpah's powers as a film-maker that even with an Olympic level drugs problem, he was able to turn moderate material into an above average thriller. Sure, some of the scenes peter out and it does occasionally resemble an episode of *Starsky & Hutch*, but the performances are uniformly excellent (Caan, Mako and Gig Young are *very* good) and while this isn't essential Peckinpah, it's still a pretty good picture. 3/5

Cross Of Iron (1977)

Cast: James Coburn (Sergeant Steiner), Maximillian Schell (Captain Stransky), James Mason (Colonel Brandt), David Warner (Captain Kiesel), Klaus Lowitsch (Kruger), Vadim Glowna (Kern), Roger Fritz (Triebeg), Dieter Schidor (Anselm), Burkhard Driest (Maag), Fred Stillkrauth (Schnurrbart), Veronique Vendell (Marga), Arthur Brauss (Zoll), Senta Berger (Eva)

Crew: Director Sam Peckinpah, Writers Julius Epstein & James Hamilton & Walter Kelley, Novel The Willing Flesh by Willi Heinrich, Producer Wolf C Hartwig, Executive Producers Arlene Sellers & Alex Winitsky, Music Ernest Gold, Cinematographer John Coquillon, Editors Michael Ellis & Tony Lawson & Herbert Taschner (uncredited), Production Designers Brian Ackland-Snow & Ted Haworth, Assistant Directors Bert Batt & Chris Carreras & Branislav Brana Srdic

Also Known As: Steiner - Das Eiserne Kreuz

Story: 1943, the Taman Peninsular and Corporal Steiner and his reconnaissance platoon return from a successful mission to find that they are under the command of a new adjutant, Captain Stransky. A Prussian aristocrat, Stransky has asked to be transferred to the Eastern Front to enhance his chances of winning the Iron Cross. He orders Steiner to shoot a young Russian boy that the platoon has taken prisoner. When Steiner refuses, the Captain flies into a rage. Eventually, one of Steiner's men, Schnurrbart, volunteers to kill to the boy. Rather than shooting the prisoner, Schnurrbart lets him hide out in the German trenches.

Stransky informs Steiner that he is now a Senior Sergeant. Nonplussed by his promotion, Steiner returns to his trench to celebrate Private Maag's birthday. Stransky, meanwhile, threatens to expose the fact that his fellow officer Triebeg is homosexual unless he supports the Captain's efforts to capture the Iron Cross.

Once the party's over, Steiner accompanies the Russian boy to the German lines and tells him to run. Before he has jogged 20 yards, the lad is gunned down by the advancing Russians. A huge battle erupts during which Steiner is injured and Stransky reveals himself to be a shameful coward.

Steiner is sent to a military hospital where he experiences terrible hallucinatory episodes. His recovery is hastened by a fling with a nurse called Eva. On learning that Schnurrbart, who was also wounded during the raid, is to return to the front line, Steiner, although still not fully fit, decides to accompany him.

The men are all delighted to see Steiner, all that is except for the company's newest member, smug SS man Zoll. Stransky is also pleased to have the Sergeant back as he hopes that Steiner will testify that it was the Captain that lead the counter-attack against the Russians. Aware that this act of bravery will secure Stransky's Iron Cross, Steiner asks the Captain why he is so desperate to win the medal. Stransky claims that he couldn't return to his family without the prize. Steiner replies that, in his opinion, Stransky doesn't deserve the Iron Cross. The Captain is all set to strike Steiner when the Russians start bombing again.

Colonel Brandt summons Steiner to a meeting to discuss Stransky's claim to the Iron Cross. The blackmailed Triebeg is also present since he has signed a form confirming that Stransky lead the counter-attack. Since everyone else says otherwise, Brandt is prepared to court-martial the Captain. Realising that it is important that the division stick together, Steiner withdraws his charge. Moments later, the Russians launch another attack and the Germans are back to battle stations.

Brandt decides that the German position is no longer tenable and orders a withdrawal. Stransky, who is left to arrange the evacuation, makes certain that Steiner's platoon don't learn of Brandt's directive, leaving the Sergeant's men at the mercy of the Russians. Although they survive a tank attack, Steiner and his troops are left stranded behind enemy lines.

As the Nazis withdraw, Steiner's men scramble for safety. At one point, the squadron think they've hit the mother lode when they encounter a farmhouse full of women, but Steiner keeps his men on a tight leash and when Zoll succumbs to his sickening sexual urges, the Sergeant insists the men move on.

Steiner's troops use every trick in the book to get within sight of the German lines. Having radioed ahead for the password, the weary platoon look certain to make it to safety. Stransky, however, believes that the radio message is part of a Russian trap and orders Triebeg to open-fire on the advancing soldiers. While his men perish around him, the seemingly invulnerable Steiner marches up to Triebeg and annihilates him with his machine-gun.

As the Russians swarm over the German encampment, Steiner goes looking for Stransky, who he finds holed up in an old factory. When Steiner goes for his machine-gun, Stransky turns his back. Rather than killing him, Steiner forces the cowardly Captain to fight alongside him. As the pair run through the factory's railway sidings, Stransky proves his ineptitude when he is unable to reload his rifle. While Stransky dodges bullets fired by a young boy, Steiner throws back his head and laughs.

And still the Russians advance...

Subtext: As Ian Johnstone wrote in the late, lamented *Neon*, *Cross Of Iron* is a film about class rather than warfare. There is little analysis of Nazi doctrine (even Stransky has few kind words for Hitler), but the film has plenty to say about the uncomfortable relationship between the aristocracy (represented by the blue-blooded Stransky in part and by the officer class in general) and the proletariat (personified by Steiner, a German so nonconformist he even speaks with an American accent).

This said, *Cross Of Iron* can also read as a fresh take on that most familiar of Peckinpah tracts, the death of the West. Men out of time, people being painted into corners by progress - *Cross Of Iron* plays a little like *The Wild Bunch*. This thematic connection is deliciously strengthened by the presence of the uniformed German officers who conspire with Mapache in Sam's ace Western.

It's also easy to appreciate why Sam, a man who spent his professional life battling producers, was completely smitten with Steiner, a soldier who seems to be at war with the entire world.

Themes & Ideas: Mirrors (Stransky is forever checking his hair), a man's best friend is his gun (Even as World War II draws to a close, the soldiers start to ready themselves for the next conflict), real men ride together (Although here we're not talking about posses but armies, brigades and battalions), ultraviolence (When Zoll forces a woman to fellate him, she responds by biting his penis off), women are trouble (Eva tries to cure Steiner of his warring ways. Zoll might argue that the women are responsible for his downfall but he really brings it on himself), friendship is a higher value that should never be betrayed but often is (although they aren't mates, Stransky and Steiner are brother soldiers, which makes the former's back-stabbing all the more difficult to forgive. Stransky also dishonours the memory of Maag by trying to take credit for the counter-attack), the law is an ass (In the midsts of war, Brandt thinks about court-martialling Stransky), revenge is bittersweet (Killing Triebeg will not bring back Steiner's platoon. Likewise, the Sergeant realises that forcing Stransky to fight is far more satisfying than mowing him down), children are lil' bastards (A Russian boy almost does for Stransky in the final scene), in the end the protagonists ride off into the sunset albeit in atypical fashion (the finale finds Steiner and Stransky running for their lives as the Russians keep on coming and coming).

Backstory: Scriptwriters James Hamilton and Walter Kelley had each seen active service, Hamilton in the trenches of Korea and Kelley during America's World War II South Pacific campaign. Fellow scribe Julius Epstein is better known for having penned *Casablanca*. Producer Wolf C Hartwig, on the other hand, is better known as the king of German soft-core pornography.

Before going on location, Peckinpah took James Coburn and the rest of the cast to Koblenz to view a pristine cut of *Triumph Of The*

Will, Leni Riefenstahl's documentary about the Nazi Party's 1934 Nuremberg Conference. "That set the tone perfectly," remembers Coburn today. "After that film we understood how these men had fallen under Hitler's spell. Hitler had taken these people on a trip, and Leni was the women who'd helped take them on it. That opening sequence, where you wait 40 minutes for Hitler's plane to arrive is amazing. You see those people looking up at the sky, looking as if they're expecting God to arrive. By the time the tri-engine lands and he steps out, you almost feel like cheering!" (A later trip to London would uncover the documentary footage that would be incorporated into *Cross Of Iron*'s opening sequence and the photographs that would be interspersed amongst the closing credits.)

Hartwig's decision to shoot *Cross Of Iron* in Yugoslavia forced the cast and crew to contend with freezing temperatures and sparse supplies. Peckinpah was particularly pissed off because he couldn't find any cocaine in Eastern Europe: he took to drinking 120 proof slivovitz instead. The producer's inability to secure much in the way of military hardware, meanwhile, meant that Sam had to create epic battle scenes with 3 rusty Russian tanks and never more than 300 costumed extras. Funds were so short, in fact, that Peckinpah ended up spending $90,000 of his own money on the picture.

According to James Coburn, when the last week of shooting arrived, Peckinpah still hadn't come up with a climax. "Arlene Sellers and Wolf Hartwig had started to panic and insisted that Sam shoot some silly little scene that they'd written. And Sam started to whine; 'They're taking it away from me! They're taking my movie away from me.' So I said; 'Get Max(imillian Schell) and let's get running!'" Scheduled for 3 days, the end sequence (in which a boy, possibly the same Russian lad we saw killed earlier, takes pot-shots at Stransky) was shot in a little over 4 hours.

As to what Sam would have made of Orson Welles' declaring *Cross Of Iron* the greatest war movie ever made, Coburn laughs: "That must have made him feel wonderful. I'm sure he had many, many drinks after hearing about that!"

Peckinpah's Posse: James Coburn delivers a perfectly nuanced performance to rival his compelling turn in *Pat Garrett And Billy The Kid*. Warner is also on top form as the dysentery-ridden, chain-smoking Captain Kiesel. And 12 years after she played a nurse in *Major Dundee*, Senta Berger appears as Eva, the Sister who has a brief fling with Steiner. On the technical side, John Coquillon weaves his usual magic with light and composition and Walter Kelley, after effortlessly stealing scenes in *Pat Garrett*, proves that he is as good at writing a script as learning one.

Reich Crispy Dialogue: i) Stransky: "What will you do when we lose the war?" Kiesel: "Prepare for the next one." ii) Steiner: "You (Brandt) think because you are more enlightened than most officers that I hate you any less? I hate all officers."

Legacy: Cross Of Iron is the only Peckinpah film to have spawned a sequel. *Sergeant Steiner* (aka *Steiner - Das Eiserne Kreuz, 2 Teil*, Dir Andrew McLaglen, 1978) starred Richard Burton, Curt Jurgens, Rod Steiger and Robert Mitchum and was a huge financial success. Seen next to Sam's brutal drama, *Sergeant Steiner* looks rather like an episode of *The A-Team*.

The Verdict: An English-language film made in Yugoslavia with an American director and German producer that tells the story of World War II from the Nazis' point of view and suggests that the Russians really won the war: it's little wonder *Cross Of Iron* performed so poorly at the American box-office. That the picture is now regarded as one of the finest war movies ever made is attributable not to its idiosyncrasies but to Sam Peckinpah's peerless direction. Coburn, Mason and Shell are the names that appear above the title, but 'Bloody Sam' is the real star of this show. It's a little ragged sometimes, as was Peckinpah when he shot it, but if you were one of those people that were shocked by *Saving Private Ryan* (1998, dir Steven Spielberg), you'll be completely blown away by *Cross Of Iron*. 4/5

Convoy (1978)

Cast: Kris Kristofferson (Rubber Duck), Ali MacGraw (Melissa), Ernest Borgnine (Lyle Wallace), Burt Young (Pig Pen), Madge Sinclair (Widow Woman), Franklyn Ajaye (Spider Mike), Brian Davies (Chuck Arnold), Seymour Cassel (Governor Haskins), Cassie Yates (Violet), Walter Kelley (Hamilton), J D Kane (Big Nasty), Billy E Hughes (Pack Rat), Whitey Hughes (White Rat), Bill Coontz (Old Iguana), Tommy J Huff (Lizard Tounge), Larry Spaulding (Bald Eagle), Randy Brady (Sneaky Snake), Allen Keller (Rosewell), James H Burk (Frick), Robert Orrison (Bookman), Tommy Bush (Chief Stacey Love), William C Jones Jnr (Fish), Jorge Russek (Tiny Alvarez), Tom Runyon (Runyon), Vera Zenovich (Thelma), Patricia Martinez (Maria), Donald R Fritts (Reverend Sloane), Bobbie Barnes, Sammy Lee Creason, Cleveland Dupin, Gerald McGee, Terry Paul, Michael Utley & Wayne D Wilkinson (Jesus Freaks), Charles Benton (Deke Thornton), George Coleman (Septic Sam), Greg Van Dyke (Silver Streak), Ed Blatchford (Roger), Paula Baldwin (Samantha), Herb Robins (Mechanic Bob), Robert J Visciglia Snr (Ice Cream Seller), Don Levy (Senator Myers), Spec O'Donnell (18 Wheel Eddie), James R Moore (Motorcycle Cop), Jim Edgecomb (Doug - Press Man), John Gill (Jack - Garage Attendant), Daniel D Halleck (Bart), Stacy Newton (Bubba), Sabra Wilson (Madge), Pepi Lenzi (News Crewman), John Bryson (Texas Governor), Sam Peckinpah (TV Newsman - uncredited)

Crew: Director Sam Peckinpah, Writer B W L Norton, Producer Robert M Sherman, Executive Producers Michael Deeley & Barry Spikings, Music C W McCall, Cinematographer Harry Stradling Jnr, Editors Graeme Clifford & Garth Craven & John Wright, Art Director J Dennis Washington, Production Designer Fernando Carrere, Set Decoration Francisco Lombardo, Costume Designers Carol & Kent James, Assistant Directors Newt Arnold & Cliff Coleman & Pepi Lenzi & John M Poer & Tom Shaw & Richard A Wells & Ron Wright

Story: After a set-to in an Arizona diner with corrupt sheriff Lyle Wallace, long-haul driver Rubber Duck makes a break for the state line, accompanied by a drifter called Melissa and some of his CB

(Citizen Band) buddies. Despite Wallace's best efforts, the truckers make it to New Mexico, where they are joined by a number of other drivers and, in no time at all, there's a mile-long convoy hauling ass towards Albuquerque.

Since Rubber Duck's rig is carrying explosive chemicals, the police are powerless to stop him. And so the convoy continues to swell. A man from the State Governor's office asks the drivers what they are protesting about. Everyone gives a different reply. As far as Rubber Duck is concerned, the purpose of the convoy is to keep on moving.

When the drivers stop to rest up for the night, Rubber Duck is visited by New Mexico Governor Haskins, who sees a chance to make political capital out of the truckers' cause. He even promises to endorse a drive all the way to the White House. Although his fellow drivers are all in favour of riding to Washington, Rubber Duck drives to Texas, where he has learnt that Wallace is holding his friend Spider Mike.

Using his rig to break into the jail, Rubber Duck frees his buddy and, with the convoy back in tow, heads for Mexico. By the time the drivers get to the border, it is being patrolled by the National Guard who have been called in by Wallace. Rubber Duck is ordered to give himself up, but he decides to rush the border. In the mêlée that follows, the Duck's truck explodes before crashing into the Rio Bravo.

Governor Haskins holds a memorial service in Rubber Duck's memory which Wallace and the drivers attend. As the service breaks up, Wallace notices a familiar face in one of the vehicles. Like the man says: "you ever seen a duck couldn't swim?"

Subtext: Convoy is a film about long distance lorry driving. Do you really think it has a subtext?

Themes & Ideas: It doesn't have too many of these, either, just some pretty standard stuff about camaraderie, changing times and the untrustworthiness of authority figures.

Backstory: It was producer Robert M Sherman who had the bright idea of transforming C W McCall's Country & Western hit into a feature film. The song is unusual since it is actually worse than 'Convoy GB,' a send-up recorded by Laurie Lingo & The Dip-sticks, alias Radio One DJs Dave Lee Travis and Paul Burnett.

Midway through the making of *Convoy*, film legend and former Peckinpah affiliate Steve McQueen showed up on set. McQueen's arrival followed a heated discussion with Sam over the director's casting of Steve's wife Ali MacGraw. (McQueen: "What the hell do you think you're doing, Sam, asking my wife to do a movie?" Peckinpah: "Steve, she's the main ingredient that will make this film legitimate." McQueen: "Yeah, well you're disrupting my home life.") The McQueen/MacGraw marriage had been in trouble for some years now, the problems in part stemming from Steve's refusal to let Ali act (before *Convoy*, the last time she'd worked was in 1971, opposite her husband in *The Getaway*). McQueen came on location not so much to be with MacGraw as to see whether the rumours about her having had an affair with one of the crew were true. Used to being at the centre of things, McQueen couldn't really deal with the attention that was being lavished on Ali. While Steve sat around the pool drinking beer, MacGraw was making more than just movies. As she would later reveal in her autobiography *Moving Pictures*: "I had had a kind of druggy affair periodically during that movie." Although he'd never managed to be faithful to any of the women he'd been out with, McQueen was appalled by MacGraw's 'betrayal' and filed for divorce the following November. Until his death in 1980, Steve McQueen never forgave Sam Peckinpah for the role he'd 'played' in destroying his marriage.

On the day *Convoy* wrapped, Sam Peckinpah commented: "I haven't done one good day's work on this whole picture." What Sam had done was expose over 800,000 feet of film. To put this in context, he shot only 300,000 feet while making *The Wild Bunch*. Even working with old friend Garth Craven, Sam couldn't edit the film down below three-and-a-half hours long. Aware that the studio wouldn't possibly release a film of that length, Sam Peckinpah did something he'd never done before: he allowed the producers to take the film away from him. Eventually released in June 1977, *Convoy* went on to gross $46.5 million in the US, making it Sam's biggest box-office hit.

Peckinpah sought to use this commercial success to adapt *Snowblind*, Robert Sabbag's account of his time spent trafficking cocaine in South America. It was a picture Sam appeared born to make; an action-packed adventure centring around a product he had tremendous faith in. In Colombia to scout locations, Peckinpah was invited to a diner at which he was to be guest of honour (Sam had been a big celebrity in Latin America ever since making *The Wild Bunch*). After the banquet, Sam was ushered into a room where he was confronted by a band of men carrying submachine-guns. The host, who also happened to run one of the biggest drugs cartels in the subcontinent, then suggested to him that making a film about the cocaine industry wasn't a very good idea. Rather than simply agreeing, Sam went into one of his screaming fits. It was a miracle that he made it back to the US alive.

Peckinpah's Posse: Besides starring, Kris Kristofferson sat in the director's chair whenever Peckinpah was too drunk to work. Donnie Fritts is also present, playing a character with the same name as David Warner's reverend in *The Ballad Of Cable Hogue* (there's also a minor character called Deke Thornton). Ali MacGraw makes her second appearance in a Peckinpah film although she's considerably less interesting than she was in *The Getaway*. As for Ernest Borgnine, it's hard to reconcile his hammy performance here with the fully-realised turn he gave in *The Wild Bunch*.

Legacy: A year after *Convoy* came out, Peckinpah played Dr Sam Collins, a lascivious gynaecologist, in Michael J Paradise's *The Visitor* (aka *Stridulum*). It was a strange role to accept given that half of Hollywood already had Sam figured as a mammoth misogynist. Since upsetting feminists gave Peckinpah the same pleasure as torturing producers, perhaps we should write the whole exercise off as a gigantic wind-up.

Even later still, in 1982, Sam did some uncredited second-unit work for his old friend Don Siegel on the action comedy *Jinxed!*.

Verdict: Sorry, Sam, but even Dysons don't suck like this. 0/5

The Osterman Weekend (1983)

Cast: Rutger Hauer (John Tanner), John Hurt (Lawrence Fassett), Craig T Nelson (Bernard Osterman), Dennis Hopper (Richard Tremayne), Chris Sarandon (Joseph Cardone), Meg Foster (Ali Tanner), Helen Shaver (Virginia Tremayne), Cassie Yates (Betty Cardone), Sandy McPeak (Stennings), Christopher Starr (Steve Tanner), Burt Lancaster (Maxwell Danforth), Cheryl Carter (Marcia Heller), John Bryson (Honeymoon Groom), Anne Haney (Honeymoon Bride), Kristen Peckinpah (Tremayne's Secretary), Marshall Ho'o (Martial Arts Instructor), Jan Triska (Mikalovich), Hansford Rowe (General Keever), Merete Van Kamp (Zuna Brickman), Bruce A Block (Floor Manager), Buddy Joe Hooker (Kidnapper), Tim Thomerson (Motorcycle Cop), Deborah Chiaramonte (Nurse), Walter Kelley (Agent #1), Brick Tilley (Agent #2), Eddy Donno (Agent #3), Dan Surles (Assailant), Janeen Davis (Stage Manager #1), Bob Kensinger (Stage Manager #2), Buckley Norris (Technician), Gregory Joe Parr (Helicopter Pilot), Don Shafer (Helicopter Agent), Irene Gorman Wright (Executive Assistant)

Crew: Director Sam Peckinpah, Writer Alan Sharp, Adaptation Ian Masters, Novel Robert Ludlum, Producers Peter S Davis & William N Panzer, Executive Producers Guy Collins & Larry N Jones & Michael T Murphy, Associate Producers Don Guest & E C Monell, Music Lalo Schifrin, Cinematographer John Coquillon, Editors Edward M Abroms & David Rawlins, Production Designer & Art Director Robb Wilson King, Set Decoration Keith Hein, Production Manager Don Guest, Assistant Directors Rodney Amateau & Laura Andrus & Win Phelps & Robert Rooy

Story: Torn apart by the murder of his wife, secret agent Lawrence Fassett dedicates himself to uncovering the Soviet Omega group. His work interests CIA Director Maxwell Danforth who hires Fassett to expose 3 Russian agents: financier Joseph Cardone; plastic surgeon Richard Tremayne; and TV writer Bernard Osterman. Fassett hopes to destroy their facade using TV presenter John Tanner, who graduated from Berkeley with the trio.

Tanner is summoned to a meeting where Fassett shows him video footage of his 3 friends in talks with their Russian contact Mikalovich. The TV host is also confronted by Danforth who convinces Tanner to let Fassett bug his house during one of the quartet's regular get-togethers, known as Ostermans. Tanner agrees on the grounds that Danforth appears on his television show.

Tanner isn't wholly convinced that his friends are international spies and he harbours doubts about letting Fassett install surveillance equipment. It's only after Mikalovich tries to abduct his wife and son that Tanner is convinced of the righteousness of Fassett's mission.

The weekend at the Tanner house commences with the friends and their partners watching a home video of a pool party. Midway through the screening, an Omega symbol appears on the screen, unsettling Cardone, Tremayne and Osterman. Tanner, meanwhile, is in the kitchen speaking with Fassett over the short-circuit television. The agent just has time to inform Tanner that he has planned a little surprise for the following evening, when Osterman and the others barge in, demanding to know where their host got the cassette tape transferred. Tanner's explanation, that he had the tape processed at the TV studios, convinces nobody.

The next day, the traditional Osterman atmosphere is further soured when Cardone and Tanner have a fight in the pool. Then, during their evening meal, Fassett uses a remote device to screen some footage about Swiss banking on the TV. Cardone, Osterman and Tremayne are visibly shaken. Tempers fray as the 3 explain to Tanner that they have been diverting funds into a secret bank account, and Ali Tanner and Virginia Tremayne exchange blows. Then, the Tanners' son, Chris, finds what he believes to be the head of his pet dog in the fridge. The head is fake, but John's fury is anything but.

Amidst the mistrust, the Cardones and Tremaynes decide to leave, but as they drive away from the compound, their RV explodes. With Ali and Chris Tanner having fled into the woods, Lawrence Fassett's men close in on the estate, intent on killing anyone they find. Osterman confronts Tanner and explains that his crimes amount to little more than illegal banking. The pair see off their attackers, only for Fassett to take Chris and Ali hostage. Tanner and Osterman now have no choice other than to participate in the agent's scheme to expose Maxwell Danforth as the man who murdered his wife.

Danforth is scheduled to appear on Tanner's TV show. Midway through the interview, the camera cuts to Fassett who outlines Danforth's high crimes. As the agent speaks, a helicopter takes off from the roof of the TV studio.

Fassett is still lambasting Danforth when none other than John Tanner bursts into his makeshift studio. The speechless Fassett tries to go for his gun, but it is too late. Tanner shoots the secret agent and frees his family.

Meanwhile, Tanner's pre-recorded broadcast draws to a close...

Subtext: The phrases 'Robert Ludlum' and 'subtext' go together about as well as Giant Haystacks and abseiling.

Themes & Ideas: It's an indication of the film's anonymity that *The Osterman Weekend* addresses none of Sam's favourite preoccupations and contains only a handful of his signature flourishes. Indeed, were it not for the superb crossbow-fuelled battle, you wouldn't know it was a Peckinpah picture at all.

Backstory: Sam was on his best behaviour throughout the making of *The Osterman Weekend*, so desperate was he to re-establish himself as a film-maker. Unfortunately, once shooting was over, Sam found himself spending several months in a suite with David Rawlins, an editor with a colossal cocaine problem. Having not had so much as a sniff during principal photography, Sam was soon wolfing down coke like never before. In his drug addled state, Sam also started to scrap with the producers. In the end, William Panzer and Peter Davis grew so sick of Peckinpah's bitching, they recut the picture behind his back.

Determined to make *The Osterman Weekend* as successful as possible, Sam agreed to go on an extensive European tour to promote the picture. Taking his attorney Joe Swindlehurst with him for company, the trip rapidly disintegrated into the sort of bender that would have intimidated even Hunter S Thomspon. Sam didn't conduct his first interview until the day before he was due to fly back to the States. Once home, however, Sam Peckinpah never drank alcohol again.

The Osterman Weekend's screenwriter Alan Sharp (who also wrote the excellent *Night Moves* for Arthur Penn) once said that Sam Peckinpah's films played like recruiting advertisements for the National Rifle Association. "That's ridiculous," responded James Coburn in a recent interview with the BBC. "After you've seen one of Sam's films, the last thing you want to do is shoot a gun or see someone get shot. Sam wasn't a violent man. He hated violence. He hated it."

Peckinpah's Posse: As it is light on Peckinpahesque posturing, *The Osterman Weekend* is also almost completely bereft of Sam's stock company. Panzer and Davis were so frightened that Peckinpah would hijack the production, they expressly forbade him from hiring his regular accomplices. Only cinematographer John Coquillon, right-hand man Walter Kelley and Sam's daughter Kirsten (who has a small role as Tremayne's secretary) were allowed on deck. It is this absence of close allies more than anything else that accounts for the film's distant quality. At least Kelley was around to make sure that Sam always had someone to go with him to the bars/brothels/coke dens/local museums.

The Verdict: Described by Peckinpah as his first exploitation movie, this isn't so much bad as bloody disappointing. Sam deserved to go out with a bigger bang. 2/5

Guns In The Afternoon

The Osterman Weekend should have been the end of the trail for Peckinpah, but it wasn't. Instead, life exploited Sam's keen work ethic to visit one last indignity upon him. Learning that there was money and opportunity in the new world of music video, Sam took a job directing promos for Julian Lennon. The two videos, for 'Too Late For Goodbyes' and 'Valotte,' weren't actually that bad. Despite heavy MTV rotation, the promos did nothing for Sam who spent his last days lamenting the fact that his last completed film was only two minutes long.

Historians and geographers have long argued about when the American Frontier closed. Some associate it with the conquest of Texas, others to the taming of Alaska. For film fans, however, the frontier died on 9 March 1984 in a hospital in Los Angeles. Distasteful as it might sound, Sam's was a merciful death for, try as he might to embrace new phenomenon like blockbusters and music videos, there was no disguising the fact that this was a world that had fallen out of love with the West and from which his closest friends had already departed. Had he lived, he may well have gone on to eke out a couple more movies but that wouldn't have been his style, Sam Peckinpah having been born to eke out nothing except the last bullet from a rapidly emptying revolver.

Reference Materials

Books

Other than the *Pocket Essential Peckinpah,* there are three other books that ought to be on every Sam fan's gift list.

Peckinpah: The Western Films- A Reconsideration by Paul Seydor, US: University of Illinois Press, Hardback, 409 pages, £18.48, ISBN: 0252022688, Paperback, 410 pages, £20.00, ISBN: 0252068351 An incredible book, made all the more remarkable by the fact that it was written by the guy who edited *Turner And Hooch*. Seydor's weighty tome contains detailed analyses of *Ride The High Country, Major Dundee, The Wild Bunch, The Ballad Of Cable Hogue* and *Pat Garrett And Billy The Kid*, together with insights into Sam's TV Westerns (there's some particularly good material on his adaptation of *Noon Wine*) and his big-screen debut, *The Deadly Companions*. Read it and then start counting the days until Seydor gets round to writing about Sam's non-Western cinema.

Sam Peckinpah: "If They Move... Kill 'Em" by David Weddle, UK: Faber & Faber, 1996, Paperback, 593 pages, £14.99, ISBN: 0571178847 Sure, it's drier than your grandmother's fruitcake, but it's the very fact that Weddle's sober prose style throws Peckinpah's self-destruction and mania into full, shocking relief that makes *"If They Move..."* such a worthwhile read. The book's other selling point is a whopping, seventy-page chapter on *The Wild Bunch*, which is excellent except that it leaves the discussion of some of Sam's other pictures frustratingly brief (*The Deadly Companions* is dealt with in the space of two pages). The biographical information is fascinating, though, and if all you're looking for is a sound study of the man and his work, you don't need to look any further.

Peckinpah: A Portrait In Montage by Garner Simmons, US: Texas Press, 1998, Paperback, 276 pages , £14.99, ISBN: 087910273X Simmons' text is by far the best film-by-film analysis on the market. Its recent reprint is some indication of just how much interest there still is in Sam's cinema.

The above are as essential as breathing. Here are some not-so-essential Peckinpah-related books.

Doing It Right: The Best Criticism On Sam Peckinpah's The Wild Bunch by Michael Bliss (editor) US: Southern Illinois University Press, 1994, Paperback, 289 pages, £12.95, ISBN: 0809318636 Did you ever want to know what the *Pig's Knuckle Alabama Post* had to say about Sam's classic Western? You can find out here. Probably.

Justified Lives: Morality & Narrative In The Films Of Sam Peckinpah by Michael Bliss, US: Southern Illinois University Press, 1993, Hardback, 353 pages, £37.50, ISBN: 0809318237 Even if you manage to get past the intimidating title, all except film students and hard-core Sam fans will be put off by Bliss' tutorial prose style. (He uses words like 'interplay' and 'intercession' as if there was some sort of EC surplus.)

Sam Peckinpah's Feature Films by Bernard Frank Dukore, US: University Of Illinois Press, 1999, Paperback, 256 pages, £17.95, ISBN: 0252068025 If this book was one of Peckinpah's movies, it'd be *Convoy*.

Savage Cinema: Sam Peckinpah And The Rise Of Ultraviolent Movies by Stephen Price, US: University Of Texas, 1998, Paperback, 282 pages, £18.95, ISBN: 0292765827 *Osterman Weekend* screenwriter Alan Sharp once said that Sam Peckinpah's films played like recruitment advertisements for the National Rifle Association. If you believe this to be true, you'll love this book. If, on the other hand, you're an evolved being, who realises that screen violence existed a long time before Sam came along (*Birth Of A Nation*, anyone?), you'll find *Savage Cinema* laughable and lamentable.

The following are currently out of print, but you might still be able to find copies in second-hand bookstores and remainder shops.

Sam Peckinpah by Doug McKinney, US: GK Hall & Co, 1979 An above average film-by-film study.

Sam Peckinpah: Master Of Violence by Max Evans, US: Dakota Press, 1972 The author of *The Hi-Lo Country* and *Castaway* spins some fine yarns about the time he spent hanging out on the set of *The Ballad Of Cable Hogue*.

Crucified Heroes: The Films of Sam Peckinpah by Sam Butler, GB: Gordon Fraser Press, 1979 Notable if only because it's the only British book in this bibliography.

Bloody Sam by Marshall Fine, US: Donald I FIne, 1991 A must for anyone who wants to read more about the whore-fucking, hard-drinking, hell-raising Sam. The *Hollywood Babylon* of this bibliography.

Horizons West by Jim Kites, US: Indiana University Press, 1969 Great if you can get hold of it, Kites' epic text is essential not only for its excellent analyses of Sam's early pictures but for its detailed look at the cinema of Budd Boetticher and Anthony Mann. Worth ransoming a family member for.

Videos

The following are either currently available in the UK or have recently been deleted, which means that you might still be able to find copies in larger video stores or bargain bins.

Ride The High Country (1962), S050850
Major Dundee (1965), CC7476, Deleted
The Wild Bunch (The Director's Cut), (1969), S001014
The Ballad Of Cable Hogue (1970), S011298
Junior Bonner (1971), SONE7425, Deleted
The Getaway (1972), S011122, Available in widescreen S015939
Pat Garrett And Billy The Kid (The Director's Cut) (1973), S050159
Bring Me The Head Of Alfredo Garcia (1974), S050870
The Killer Elite (1975), S051304
Cross Of Iron (1977), S038005, Available in widescreen S038379
Convoy (1978), S038192
The Osterman Weekend (1983), QS127

DVDs

The Wild Bunch (*The Director's Cut*), (1969) - note, this is an essential purchase since it also includes Paul Seydor's superb, Oscar-nominated documentary *The Wild Bunch: An Album In Montage.*

The Getaway (1972) D011122

Peckinpahesque Pictures

Although everyone from Martin Scorsese to Quentin Tarantino has praised his work, of the directors working today only Walter Hill, Peckinpah's friend and working partner, has actively incorporated Sam's techniques and philosophy into his own cinema.

Hill's most Peckinpahesque picture is *The Long Riders*. A study of the infamous James/Younger gang, the picture takes several of Sam's favourite themes (betrayal, honour, camaraderie, men out of time, etc.) and sandwiches them between two awesome set pieces; the first clearly inspired by the bunkhouse shoot-out from *Pat Garrett And The Billy The Kid*, the second (Hill's re-enactment of the Great Northfield Minnesota Raid) not unlike the opening massacre of *The Wild Bunch*. Hill's other Westerns also smack of Sam: *Wild Bill* feels like a light version of *Pat Garrett* while *Geronimo - An American Legend* plays like an undernourished *Major Dundee*. And he has also incorporated elements of Sam's cinema into *The Driver*, a *Dundee*-style story of obsession, *Southern Comfort,* a professional soldier picture along *Cross Of Iron* lines, and *Another 48 Hours*, which is a great big pile of crap just like *Convoy*.

By the way, for those of you that think John Woo is a Peckinpahesque director, forget it. Woo is a talented director of flashy, lightweight action films. Peckinpah is one of this century's great chroniclers of American masculinity. The only thing that unites them is their shared love of slow motion.

Peckinpah On The Web

Sam would probably be delighted to learn that he hasn't made too big an impact on something as newfangled as the Internet. Of the few sites dedicated to the director and his work, the following are the best of the bunch.

The Films Of Sam Peckinpah: http://www.geocites.com - A charming little site featuring appraisals of all Sam's pictures as well as interviews with Paul Seydor and Arthur Schneider (the editor of *Noon Wine*), an extensive image bank and a hotchpotch of reviews and essays.

The Wild Bunch: http://www.ukonline.co.uk/wildbunch/frame.htm - Profiles of the director and all the key players, reviews, film and audio clips, stills. The sort of comprehensive, well-researched database this great movie deserves.

Sam Peckinpah: http://www.torget.se/users/b/benson13/sam.htm - A sparse, seldom-updated site redeemed by a rare magazine interview, a thorough filmography and some rather nice oak-panelled wallpaper.

The Essential Library

Enjoyed this book? Then try some other titles in the Essential library.

New This Month: **Steve McQueen** by Richard Luck
Sam Peckinpah by Richard Luck

New Next Month: **Jane Campion** by Ellen Cheshire
Krzysztof Kieslowski by Monika Maurer

Also Available:

Film: **Woody Allen** by Martin Fitzgerald
Jackie Chan by Michelle Le Blanc & Colin Odell
The Brothers Coen by John Ashbrook & Ellen Cheshire
Film Noir by Paul Duncan
Terry Gilliam by John Ashbrook
Heroic Bloodshed edited by Martin Fitzgerald
Alfred Hitchcock by Paul Duncan
Stanley Kubrick by Paul Duncan
David Lynch by Michelle Le Blanc & Colin Odell
Brian De Palma by John Ashbrook
Vampire Films by Michelle Le Blanc & Colin Odell
Orson Welles by Martin Fitzgerald

TV: **The Slayer Files: Buffy the Vampire Slayer** by Peter Mann
Doctor Who by Mark Campbell
The Simpsons by Peter Mann

Books: **Stephen King** by Peter Mann
Noir Fiction by Paul Duncan

Available at all good bookstores at £2.99 each, or send a cheque to:
Pocket Essentials (Dept SP), 18 Coleswood Rd, Harpenden, Herts, AL5 1EQ, UK Please make cheques payable to 'Oldcastle Books.' Add 50p postage & packing for each book in the UK and £1 elsewhere.

US customers can send $5.95 plus $1.95 postage & packing for each book to **Trafalgar Square Publishing, P.O. Box 257, Howe Hill Road, North Pomfret, Vermont 05053, USA**. tel: 802-457-1911, fax: 802-457-1913, e-mail: tsquare@sover.net

Customers worldwide can order online at **www.pocketessentials.com**, **www.amazon.com** and at all good online bookstores.